Italian Food Rules

by
Ann Reavis

ITALIAN FOOD RULES

ISBN 13: 978-1512188646
ISBN 10: 1512188646

Cover by: Kelly Crimi

Interior book design by Bob Houston eBook Formatting

Email: italianfoodrules@gmail.com

Second Edition (June 1, 2015)

DEDICATION

To Francesca, who knows and follows all of the
Italian Food Rules.

CONTENTS

FOREWORD

It is a joy to learn something new and surprising. As a teacher, it is even better when I learn from a student.

Ann Reavis, a San Francisco lawyer in search of any enlightenment that nine months in Italy could bring her, walked into my Italian grammar class in Massa Marittima, near the Tuscan coast, in 1998. To be kind, let's say that she had no ear for my melodic language.

Changing focus, she sought to learn to expand her kitchen skills beyond admittedly delicious chocolate chip cookies and carrot cake to include Florentine and Tuscan recipes. I was conducting cooking classes for Americans and other tourists. Ann, unfortunately, could never master a passable *soffritto* or achieve *al dente* when it came to cooking pasta.

I was ready to give up on the notion that Ann was ever going to awaken to the state of being Italian even for a day, but then we started to delve into the customs and practices that make Italian food authentic. Maybe it is the lawyer's need for defined rules and precedents, or Ann's love for research that, combined with her passion for eating, if not cooking, Italian food led her to collect what she came to call "Italian Food Rules."

After nine months in Florence became over fifteen years in Italy, Ann is still clearly American, but she knows more than most Italians about the basis of the food practices that are passed down from generation to generation. Her delight in each discovery has frequently been shared in her writing on TuscanTraveler.com and, now, in this enchanting book.

The facts, fictions, history and reasons behind the Italian Food Rules, as well as the revelation of the mere existence of so many customs or edicts, will assist any visitor to Italy by making their stay easier, less confusing, and richer. For Italians, their response to reading Ann's list of the rules is usually *"giusto, giusto"* ("exactly right") and then delight when they read the rationale and history of the gastronomic commandments passed down from their grandmothers.

I never knew where Caesar Salad originated (certainly not Italy), or why spaghetti with meatballs was considered an Italian dish, or why Americans always wanted a bowl of olive oil with a squiggle of balsamic vinegar delivered immediately to the table when dining at a trattoria. I enjoy eating *lampredotto* and *lardo* on a regular basis, being very familiar with these Tuscan specialties, but I never thought much about their origins in Italian history until Ann started asking questions, urging me to translate at Florentine tripe stands, and traveling to Colonnata to see where herbed lard is aged.

The bricks that form the foundation of the most loved cuisine in the world today are important and should be preserved. Ann Reavis has given us the gift of memory in her light and amusing book of Italian Food Rules.

Francesca Maria Boni, Florence

By Way of Introduction

In Italy they love making rules, and they obey very few…except when it comes to food. The Italian Food Rules may as well be carved in marble. They will not change and you violate them at your peril.

I grew up during the '50s in the American West where there were no food rules. TV dinners vied with Chef Boyardee canned spaghetti and meatballs. Sweet potatoes were topped with marshmallows. A fried egg smothered in ketchup or a breakfast burrito was equally good in the morning. Iced tea paired well with any food. A Filet O'Fish, French fries, and a Big Gulp were road food–better tasting eaten in the car, than out.

Then I moved to San Francisco and my junk food days were over. Now I was dining on all of the fine cuisines of the world, including at some of the best Italian restaurants in America. (Full disclosure: I still scarfed down the occasional pint of ice cream for dinner.)

I thought I knew Italian cuisine when I arrived

in Italy in 1998 for what turned out to be a fifteen-year sojourn. I may have been able to recognize Italian food, but I had no clue about the Italian Food Rules. I broke every single one of them.

The Italian Food Rules have a long history. Some traveled with Catherine de' Medici to France in the 16th century. Others are even older.

Despite the attempts by outsiders to influence the politics and cultural life of the Italian peninsula for the past millennium, the Italian people have remained largely homogenous. They will argue there are insurmountable regional differences in their recipes, but outsiders will be hard pressed to understand what all the fuss is about. Since Italians do not generally move far from home, the food traditions are passed on unchanged from generation to generation. Italian Food Rules practiced 200 years ago are still valid today.

The Italian food culture encourages eating foods that are in season and grown locally, which could be considered two of the most important Italian Food Rules. It is little wonder that the Slow Food movement started in Italy.

Founded in 1989 in the Piemonte region to counter the rise in Italy of fast food, the organization's interests grew to include the disappearance of local food culture and traditional ingredients. Slow Food is now a grassroots organization with over 100,000 supporters in 150 countries around the world, who are linking the pleasure of good food with a commitment to their community and the environment. The organization's philosophy has its basis in the Italian Food Rules.

This small book just skims the surface of the Italian Food Rules. Although some Italians might rightly argue that one or two of these Rules don't apply to their region or their small town, this book is meant to be of some assistance to the visitor who wants to try to be Italian at least once in a lifetime.

DON'T DRINK CAPPUCCINO AFTER TEN IN THE MORNING

To order a cappuccino after lunch is a direct and major violation of an Italian Food Rule. Italians believe the fresh whole milk that makes up over half of the contents of cappuccino plays havoc with digestion. To order a cappuccino after 10am, unless you are breakfasting after said hour, is seen as suspect behavior worthy of at least a slight frown, advancing to a worried shake of the head, and can escalate to outright ridicule.

To the Italians, milk is almost a meal in itself. So having a cappuccino at the neighborhood bar in the morning on the way to work or school requires no other food to be considered a complete breakfast. (A small pastry may be included, but not always.) Cappuccino is more milk than coffee, so it is full of calories. Perhaps the reasoning is that slender Italians (the ones who don't order the pastry) are more likely to burn off the calories through the day. Drunk later, those pesky calories stay on the hips.

Some say that cappuccino is best in the morning because the milk has lactose (a sugar) and the body absorbs the lactose and milk fat quickly, so the carbohydrate energy is available immediately before the caffeine stimulant kicks in.

The real reason behind the Food Rule, however, is that Italians are firmly convinced that drinking milk after any meal will mess up the stomach's ability to digest food properly. So having a cappuccino at any time after lunch, or after dinner, in Italy is unthinkable.

Tourists, therefore, shouldn't be shocked when the waiter refuses to grant their cappuccino requests "for your own health."

DID YOU KNOW?

- No slice of lemon or lemon peel with espresso.
- If you must have milk in your after-meal coffee, order *caffè macchiato* (stained coffee).
- Coffee can be served with a shot of alcohol (grappa, cognac, rum), order *caffè corretto*.
- There are no frappuccinos in Italy, order *caffè shakerato*.
- *Caffè* is to be drunk standing at a bar or at the table after a meal.
- Italians do not order double espresso—espresso is a short drink.

Don't Ask For Half & Half or Soy Milk For Your Coffee

Is it a sign of the end of culture when the choices, or individual demands, get too numerous? The babel of maladies, desires, and requests bombard us— "I'm lactose intolerant. Do you have lactose-free milk or soy?" "I want just the essence of coffee, can you add more cream, or, better yet, whipped cream?" "I'm on a diet—skim milk, please." "I want whole milk—cold." "I want Half & Half—do you know what that is—like, half cream, half milk? It sometimes comes in a tiny plastic container, back home?"

Coffee is simple in Italy. You can find it the following ways in any coffee bar:

un caffè—this is a single-shot espresso, but don't call it espresso, no Italian does. Do not order *un caffè doppio*—a double espresso or wait a couple of hours, as the Italians do, for your next dose.

cappuccino and *caffellatte*—before 10am.

caffè macchiato or *latte macchiato*–an espresso with a dash of milk or a hot milk with a dash of coffee (remember, mornings only).

caffè corretto–the Italian male's (gender specific and usually of the blue–collar variety) early morning pick-me-up, an espresso "corrected" with a shot of brandy or grappa.

caffè freddo or *cappuccino freddo*–iced espresso or cappuccino, possibly with sugar added by the barista.

un caffè lungo or *un caffè ristretto*–more or less water in an *espresso*) or ask for an *americano* if you want the traditional cup o' joe.

There are a couple of regional exceptions. In Naples, the locals order un *caffè alla nocciola*–a frothy espresso with hazelnut cream. In Milan, the fashionistas ask for *un marocchino*, an upside-down *cappuccino*, served in a small glass that is first sprinkled with cocoa powder, then hit with a bit of frothed milk, then finished off with a shot of espresso.

Don't Ask For Coffee "To Go"

It is a simple joy for many Americans to begin their multi-tasking day with a long coffee "to go." They prepare the brew in their own special way and pour it into a hi-tech stainless steel sippy cup that fits perfectly in the cup holder of their SUV. Or they stop a block from the office, pull out their Starbucks Reward Card and continue down the street scalding their palate with that first impatient sip.

Think of the overwhelming joy of American commuters when Starbucks and Dunkin' Donuts put in drive-through windows.

Italians don't believe in delayed gratification. Their morning *cappuccino* or afternoon *espresso* must be made with perfectly ground, roasted Arabica coffee beans from the doser grinder, tamped into the filter basket of a properly pre-heated Italian-made coffee machine by a *barista* who has been doing the same repetitive action for 20 years. Italians will immediately drink the *espresso* (three sips) or *cappuccino* (ten sips) from the appropriate sized ceramic cup while standing at the bar where their fathers and grandfathers stood before them.

Some Italians have never sipped a coffee outside of a coffee bar—not at home, or a friend's home, and certainly not out of a paper cup. The only exception for these hard-liners is a very occasional *espresso* at the end of a meal in a restaurant.

The basis of the Food Rule is quality—of the coffee bean, the coffee machine, the cup and the *barista*. This assures the consistent temperature, the appropriate strength, the correct amount (never a double *espresso*), and the right amount and temperature of any added milk (a few drips for a *macchiato* and never "extra cream" for a *cappuccino*).

The experience is immediate and satisfying. If one part of the process goes awry the whole day could be ruined.

ITALIANS ONLY DRINK TEA WHEN THEY ARE SICK

Tea drinkers of the U.K. and the U.S. might as well give up the idea of a good "cuppa" in Italy. Italians only drink tea when they are sick–at home.

You can ask for, and receive, hot tea in a coffee bar. First, the *barista* will give you a searching glance from a distance to see if you are obviously infectious. Then, he will run some hot water out of the coffee machine into a *cappuccino* cup. The water will be unfiltered tap water, which may taste great, but in Florence, for example, is highly mineralized, a taste hidden easily by coffee, but not by tea. And, having passed through the coffee machine, the water will have the odor, if not the taste, of stale coffee.

The water may or may not be of sufficient temperature to brew tea from the generic tea bag (or, perhaps, Lipton or Twinings in an upscale bar). The tea bag will be wrapped in its paper cover, resting in the saucer of the rapidly cooling cup of water.

If you go out to dinner at the home of an Italian friend, carry your own tea bags. Their cupboards will only contain chamomile tea bags or *tisane della salute*. Also, be prepared for the sympathetic look and an inquiry about how long you have been feeling "under the weather." Finally, your friends may not have cups for tea, only tiny cups for espresso. A water glass can substitute for a teacup, but don't fill it too full, only the top edge will stay cool enough to touch.

As for your own vacation rental in Italy: plan to bring an electric kettle, a Brita pitcher with filters, and your favorite tea. In cities, specialty grocery stores will carry good tea, but at high prices.

Get used to the question "*Prendiamo un caffè?*" and the look you will get when you say you drink tea. As a foreigner, you will be given a pass. Imagine a tea-loving, coffee-hating Italian–his life would be like being a vegetarian at a Texas barbecue...every single day of the year.

DON'T DIP BREAD IN OLIVE OIL

It was over twenty years ago when I first broke the Italian Food Rule: Don't Dip Bread in Olive Oil. Or, to clarify: Don't serve bread with a bowl of olive oil with a swirl of balsamic vinegar as an appetizer (or any other part of the meal).

Back to my first experience: I was trying a new restaurant in San Francisco. I watched with curiosity as our waiter presented with a flourish a thin sliced baguette of warm sourdough bread and a bowl of deep green extra virgin olive oil. But he didn't stop there. With some sleight of hand, he then produced a small bottle of balsamic vinegar and created a floating purplish *S* on the surface of the oil.

Noting our bemused expressions, he explained that the proper procedure was to dip a bite of torn bread into the oil, catching a smidgen of the *aceto balsamico* (I can't remember if he actually said "*aceto balsamico*") and pop it into one's mouth. I caught on immediately and, for the next five years or so, I savored bread dipped in olive oil throughout the fine restaurants of San Francisco and across the United States.

In 1998, I arrived in Italy and it was immediately apparent that there was absolutely no practice of setting bowls of olive oil on the table so customers could munch on bread before the *antipasti* arrived. In fact, then and now, there may not be bread on the table until the main course is served (see Don't Eat Bread with Pasta).

However, by the turn of the millennium, most Americans, including those from places like Iowa and Texas, were hooked on olive oil and bread. They arrived in droves on Italian shores expecting to be served olive oil, bread, and even, that squiggle of balsamic vinegar, in the trattorias and fine restaurants across Italy.

In the beginning, Italian waiters (and restaurant owners) were simply confused—why all of this demand for olive oil when there was no food on which to put it? But then they swiftly moved from being perplexed to being appalled.

Why appalled, you ask? Certainly Americans (and tourists of all nationalities) had broken Italian Food Rules before, but those infractions paled in comparison with what happened when Americans, olive oil, and bread were combined. It was a catastrophe: A tourist asks for bread. The waiter complies, sneering a bit because he knows that eating bread before a meal ruins the appetite and leads to fat. Then the tourist throws the waiter an impatient look and asks for the olive oil.

Now the waiter quits sneering. He either says that there is no olive oil for the dining room (salads are dressed in the kitchen; pasta and veggies get their last splash from the chef; same with the main courses). Or, he brings a large bottle of olive oil–from the kitchen or the waiters' service stand–to the table.

You say you don't understand the problem? Imagine the table in our hypothetical trattoria. Now there is a basket of bread and a bottle of olive oil in the center by the small candle or tiny floral center-piece. There are four paper placemats, each topped with a knife and fork and a napkin. What do the Americans do? They have stretched to ask for *pane* and *olio*, using the right words. They have no further language resources or patience for *piatto* (plate), and *ciotolina* or *piccola ciotola* (little bowl), or any other tableware word, and frankly they are a bit miffed that the olive oil didn't come served in a bowl.

So they take a slice of bread, place it on their paper placemat, and gingerly aim the spout of the large olive oil bottle at the center, trying desperately not to run over the crusty edges. Of course, the olive oil, poured by even the most careful person, soaks through the light Italian bread, onto the placemat or napkin underneath.

The tourist is upset and embarrassed, and the waiter is appalled and apoplectic. Now, add a cotton tablecloth under our hypothetical placemats and you see how the problem escalates. I do not exaggerate here for effect. I have seen both situations with my own eyes.

There are a few good reasons for the Italian Food Rule: Don't Dip Bread in Olive Oil. Fine Italian extra virgin olive oil–the only type to eat with bread–is expensive. To place a bowl of olive oil on the table in front of Italians guarantees the waste of excess oil because Italians don't eat bread before they start their meal. (Some might argue that Americans will wipe the bowl clean, but remember Italian Food Rules were not created with Americans in mind.) Italians, also, aren't given to eating out of a communal bowl (dipping a hunk of bread in olive oil, taking a bite and then dipping it back in the same oil would cause an Italian to go pale with visions of bacteria). There is, also, the possibility of drips. Italians avoid potential messes. This list probably just skims the surface of the reasons behind the Rule.

As for that *S* of *aceto balsamico* floating on the oil…there is probably an extra penalty for adding that to the crime. Italians do not put balsamic vinegar on bread. Italians do not make a salad dressing with balsamic vinegar and olive oil (red wine vinegar only). Traditional *aceto balsamico* is wildly expensive, exquisitely good and should never be wasted or drowned in olive oil.

But if oil and bread are so good together, why don't the Italians give in? Well, Italians do eat bread with extra virgin olive oil on top. The dish is called *fettunta* from *fetta* (slice) and *unta* (oily)–an "oily slice". The bread is not dipped in oil. A slice of bread is toasted (preferably over a flame), rubbed while still warm with a halved clove of fresh garlic, and placed on a plate. Fresh extra virgin olive oil is poured over the slice of bread and salt is added to taste. It is difficult to find this dish in a restaurant because it is considered simple home food, not worthy of a dining experience and difficult to price since it is basically a slice of bread with a splash of olive oil.

When in Italy, save the dipping of bread in olive oil for a formal tasting of the year's new oil in December and January where the purpose is not to eat a lot of bread, but just to taste a variety of fabulous extra virgin olive oils. Keep the practice out of your Italian restaurant experience, entirely.

MEAL TIME RULES

You won't find a sit-down breakfast of eggs and bacon anywhere in Italy, outside of a hotel. But you also won't be constrained by time, if you want to eat an Italian breakfast–a *cappuccino* and a pastry–while standing up at a coffee bar. Anytime between 7am and noon will work.

The majority of eating establishments that serve lunch at the table do not start seating customers until 12:30pm. (At noon you will probably find the kitchen staff and waiters enjoying their meal.) Italians eat lunch between 12:30 and 2pm. Most will be done by 2:30pm

Most restaurants and trattorias not only have specific opening times, but you can count on them closing close in the afternoon, refusing new customers after 2:30pm. If you have a late breakfast, visit museums through lunch and hope to get a bite to eat at 2pm or 3pm, you will be eating wilted salad or dried out *panini* or worse–pre-cooked spaghetti–at a self-serve cafeteria.

Dinner is a little different. The further south you go, the later Italians start eating. A Tuscan might consider dining at 8pm, but a Roman won't sit down before 9pm, and a Neapolitan is rarely ready to dine before 10pm. Restaurants will not start serving dinner anywhere in Italy before 7:30pm. Pizzerias start even later. But the good news is that you can stay late into the night, unlike in the U.S. or the U.K. where the owner wants to close up by 10pm.

DID YOU KNOW?

Artisanal gelaterias are where the Italians purchase a cone of fresh-made gelato—the only kind worth eating. Because the *gelataio* is making the ice cream in the morning, the gelateria will not open before 11am. If you see gelato available for sale before 11am, you can be sure it was not made in-house. (Note also the Italian Food Rule: Italians Don't Snack. In Italy, gelato is rarely consumed before the 4pm *merenda* that helps refresh Italians so they can make it to the 8:30pm dinner hour.)

RULES OF THE MENU

Menus in Italy are unique, uniform and sometimes a source of confusion to visitors. In no other country in the world is there such a consistent offering: *antipasti* (appetizers), *primi* (pasta, risotto and soups), *secondi* (main meat and vegetarian dishes), *contorni* (side dishes of vegetables, beans, simple salads and potatoes), and *dolce* (dessert).

Tourists frequently ask: "Do I have to order something from each section?" or "Can I get a side of pasta?" or "Why don't they bring the food we ordered all at the same time?"

Except for at special celebrations or formal dinners, Italian rarely order an *antipasto*, *primo*, *secondo*, *contorno* and *dolce* at one meal. More often they will combine a pasta and a salad and a dessert. Or they will ask for an appetizer and a main dish, perhaps followed by some fruit.

One of the Italian Food Rules holds that pasta is not a side dish. As a *primo*, it is served before the main dish, by itself. But if you only want a small portion of pasta, ask for *una mezza porzione*. You will get a half-order of pasta that will be served before the main course.

After the pasta is finished, the bowls and silverware will be replaced. A spot of pasta sauce will never touch the veal chop you ordered. Likewise, side dishes of fried potatoes or Tuscan white beans or sautéed spinach will be served on separate plates from your main dish. Think of a six-year-old in distress: "But my mashed potatoes are *touching* the fried chicken." Italians refuse to allow the flavor of one dish to invade the taste of another.

As for timing, the menu will help you to avoid the problem frequently faced by unknowing tourists when one orders a pasta and the other orders a main dish. The waiter brings the pasta first and then fifteen minutes later brings the main dish, leaving each person to eat alone as the other looks on. Solve this problem by simply asking the waiter to bring both dishes "*insieme*" (together).

Keep in mind the following: *antipasti* usually take 3 to 5 minutes to prepare; a *primo* can take up to 15 minutes (more for a risotto, but the menu will usually say so), and a *secondo* will usually take 20 minutes or more unless it is a slice off a roast, like *arista* (pork roast). So if one person wants *ravioli* (*primo*) and a salad (*contorno*), while her friend wants bruschetta (*antipasto*) and *Bistecca alla Fiorentina* (*secondo*) and they tell their waiter to bring them *insieme*, the salad and *bruschetta* will arrive first. The chef will know to put the steak on the grill before the *ravioli* go into boiling water. Just as the steak is finishing, the *ravioli* get their five minutes to cook and be sauced. Both dishes come to the table together.

The timing information inherent in the menu can also help you plan the length of a meal. In a hurry? Order a pasta and salad. Want a long relaxed meal under the stars? Savor some of the more complex dishes that you will never cook at home. Good Italian food is cooked to order from fresh ingredients. It takes time to prepare and deserves to be savored in a leisurely manner.

DID YOU KNOW?

• A waiter will never tell you that he "needs your table".

• The check will never be placed on your table until you ask for it (unless it is after midnight).

• It will take at least 15 to 30 minutes to get your bill once you ask for it.

• Tipping is optional.

• Take twice as much time to enjoy eating a meal, as it took to cook.

• *A tavola non s'invecchia* (At the table you do not age).

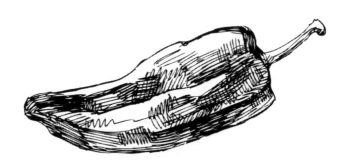

NO PIZZA FOR LUNCH

"*Mangiare la pizza prima delle nove mi fa tristezza,*" say Italians everywhere. "To eat pizza before 9pm makes me sad."

Pizza is eaten in the U.S. at any time of the day–even cold for breakfast in dorm rooms on every college campus. Italians refuse to eat food served any which way, at any time of day or night.

According to the Italian Food Rule, pizza is to be eaten at a pizzeria at night because: 1) pizza must be made to order (no frozen pizza); 2) pizza must be eaten immediately after it comes out of the pizza oven (no take-out); 3) pizza must be made by an expert–not just any old cook–a *pizzaiolo* (preferably born in Naples), who 4) is using a wood-burning pizza oven.

A wood-burning pizza oven takes a long time to get to the proper temperature (485° C or 905° F), so it will not produce the perfect pizza before 8:30 or 9 in the evening and it is usually considered a waste of time and energy (as well as a violation of the Food Rule) to fire it up for lunch. Pizzerias stay open until midnight or later, so a *pizzaiolo* gets in a full shift of work from prep at 7pm to clean-up at 1am.

Another reason for the Food Rule is that pizza, unlike pasta, is considered a social food—a food for lovers and friends—not so often for a family outing. Pasta is associated with home cooking. Traditionally, Italians were expected home for lunch for pasta. When both parents started working outside the home, the pasta meal moved to dinner.

Since the perfect pizza can't be made at home (no kitchen oven reaches 485° C and most of the private wood-burning pizza ovens built in Italy are installed at the request of foreigners who want a "true Italian experience" at their vacation villa or Tuscan farmhouse), it becomes a social event. Pizzerias provide an upbeat, carefree, casual environment where the wood-burning pizza oven is on display, as is the *pizzaiolo*, adding to the festive atmosphere.

DID YOU KNOW?

• Eat pizza with a fork and knife (unless you are a guy *and* you are in Naples).
• Drink beer or *acqua frizzante* with pizza (Coke and Fanta, if you are under 25 years old).
• Pizza may be eaten by the slice, late at night, while standing, in a *pizza al taglio* place.
• It is sad to eat pizza alone.

FOR PIZZA, ONE SIZE FITS ALL

Italians are not inclined to share food from plate to plate, meaning they don't take tastes, bites, or portions off each other's *pasta alle vongole* or veal chops. Therefore, there is no practice of ordering an extra large pizza for four people to share. Even two people don't share a pizza. One person, one pizza.

There are many reasons for this: hygiene, esthetics, topping choice, and pizza-eating style.

Throughout the Italian Food Rules the fear of germs is the major rationale for the rule: don't dip bread in a communal bowl of olive oil, no touching the vegetables at the market, etc. Although a shared pizza can be a virus-free act if the knife and fork skills of the participants are honed and the transfer of the slices to individual plates are handled smoothly, but then you have the problem of esthetics.

The tables in a pizzeria (you, of course, would not order a pizza anywhere else other than a pizzeria) tend to be on the small size. Therefore, a large pizza in the center of the table (displacing the candle) and individual plates in front of each diner is just not the right look, too cramped. Add beer glasses, cutlery, placemats, napkins and the condiment (*peperoncino* only) and you've got a mess. Much better to have the place settings, candle, beer, and a same-sized pizza on its own plate in front of each diner. Festive and balanced.

Probably most important reason for individual pizzas is that underlying rational of almost all Italian Food Rules—there is to be no mixing of flavors (pasta is not a side dish, no all-you-can-eat buffets, separate plates for *contorni*, etc.). Pizzas in Italy max out at about four ingredients. Even when you order a *quattro stagioni* (four seasons), each of the ingredients has its own quarter of the pizza. They do not overlap. There is no Italian pizza with "everything on it."

The pizzas described on the menu are chosen with care. The flavor meld harmoniously: *Margherita* with tomato sauce, mozzarella and one basil leaf; *Marinara* with tomato sauce, garlic and oregano; *Diavola* with tomato sauce, mozzarella and spicy salami; and *Napoletana* with tomato sauce, mozzarella, anchovies and capers, to describe a few of the classic styles. Don't ask for half *Vegetariana*, half *Diavola* or *Marinara* with mozzarella cheese (the garlic conflicts with the mozzarella). If the flavors or ingredients do not go together in any other Italian dish, they will not be considered appropriate for a pizza.

The size of an Italian pizza is time-tested and perfect for one person with little to none left over at the end (uneaten pizza is not boxed up for leftovers). The *pizzaiolo* makes one-sized yeasty dough balls in the morning that rise during the day, perfect for making hundreds of same-sized pizzas after 8:30pm (pizza is never eaten for lunch) in a wood-burning pizza oven.

People have their own preference for how to eat their own pizza–another reason for not sharing. Some Italians, the majority, choose to eat with a knife and fork. But where one person will eat from the crust in, another might start in the center of a slice and eat out, saving the crust to last. A few Italians (men in Naples) will pick up a slice with their fingers and fold it slightly for better management while eating from the point out. Finally, a style of starting with knife and fork and savoring the last crusty bits with fingers is gaining a strong following. Can you imagine the havoc caused by two people with different pizza-eating styles sharing one pizza, even if they could agree on the toppings?

Enjoy your pizza Italian style: at night, in a pizzeria with a wood-burning pizza oven and a *pizzaiolo napoletano*, after ordering one of the classic combinations to be delivered hot on its own warm ceramic plate with a cold glass of beer. You, too, will eat the whole thing and enjoy it more than any other pizza; before or since.

Pizza Topping Rules

If you are not from Italy, you might think there are lots of condiments you can add to your pizza to make it "better." You are wrong. The only permissible condiment is hot chili flakes (*peperoncino*) to make a spicier pizza. Otherwise, leave the pizza the way the *pizzaiolo* intended it and just slice it and eat it as fast as possible. (Sometimes, hot chili flakes are not available and a *peperoncino* infused olive oil is offered as a substitute. It is not as good, but it is acceptable under the Italian Food Rules.)

Do not ask for grated Parmesan or garlic salt or salt or fresh cracked black pepper. Only hot chili flakes, nothing more.

As for any confusion about toppings—remember that Italians never eat pizza with "everything" on it. The ingredients will number four or less. Anything else is an exaggeration.

Mozzarella is the most common cheese for pizza, but it is usually used sparingly—asking for extra mozzarella will throw the texture and flavor of your pizza out of balance. Mozzarella from water buffalo (*mozzarella di bufala*) if cooked on a pizza will make it soggy; if crumbled on afterwards, it's a refreshing summer-time pizza.

If you want what is known in the U.S. as "pep-peroni", ask for a *pizza con salame piccante*. "*Peperone*" in Italian is the name for bell pepper, served on *pizza vegetariana*.

There will be no pineapple in an Italian pizze-ria, unless it is served, fresh-sliced, for dessert.

Don't Put Ice Cubes in Beverages

Imagine you and an Italian friend are in a New York restaurant where "Hi! I'm Sam, your waiter" is assisting you to have the *best* lunch experience possible. This includes large glasses of iced water that arrive immediately on the table with a huge basket of warm bread. Guaranteed, your Italian friend will immediately start scooping out the cubes into the empty wine glass.

"Hi! I'm Sam" arrives to take your order and notices the half-full glass of iceless water. He leaves and returns with the water pitcher, which he turns sideways so that it dispenses the maximum amount of ice and a lesser amount of water. Duty done, he grins, "Now, what sounds good to you all, today?"

Italian Food Rule: No ice cubes in beverages. Ice in Italy is to keep fresh fish fresh. Full stop.

The most common reason Italians (and other Europeans) cite for the rule is that icy cold liquids are bad for your digestion. They can even cause the dreaded *congestione*–an abdominal cramp–that can kill you.

The next frequently cited reason is a fear of the tap water used for making ice. Despite the fact that Italy has very safe tap water–not always the best tasting, but safe to drink in any form–the rate of consumption of bottled water (at room temperature) in Italy is one of the highest in Europe.

No hotel in Italy will have an ice machine in the hall and few will deliver ice to the room upon request. This may be for the reasons stated above or because ice machines use a lot of very expensive electricity and are breeding grounds of all sorts of molds, fungi, and bacteria.

Italy is a land of simple drinks–wine, beer and water (*frizzante* or *naturale*)–none of which require ice. There is not a big cocktail tradition in Italy, but in a nod to the customs of the rest of the world you will frequently find three cubes of ice floating in your Negroni.

When visiting Italy, try following the Italian Food Rule: No ice cubes in beverages. You may find that you can actually taste what you are drinking.

WITH MEALS, DRINK WATER OR WINE, NOTHING ELSE

In thousands of kitchens across America there is a person standing in front of an open fridge calling out to those gathered around the dinner table: "I've got white wine, red wine, ice tea, mango juice, beer, milk, Pellegrino, Coke, 7-Up, a bottle of Bacardi Breezer Lemon, and, of course, iced cold tap water. What does each of you want to drink?" This would never happen in an Italian kitchen.

In the homes and good restaurants of Italy the only beverages served with lunch or dinner are wine (red, white, rosé or Prosecco) and water (*frizzante* (carbonated) or *naturale* (still/no gas)). The water glasses, of course, have no ice in them.

It does not matter how young or old an Italian is: it's wine or water, only. Children sometimes have a splash of wine in their fizzy water. This practice provides them with the idea that the smart way to drink wine is in moderation.

Even adults, on a hot day, might opt for this

refreshing combo by pouring a small amount of an inexpensive Chianti into a glass of ice-free *acqua frizzante*. This is not the sweet wine cooler found on picnic tables on the 4th of July. It is a sugar-free slightly flavored glass of water.

For children and adults, alike, milk is not an option (see the Italian Food Rule on drinks such as *caffellatte* and *cappuccino*). Italian mothers will tell you how milk interferes with a person's digestion.

Italians never drink coffee with food during a meal. It is sipped from tiny *espresso* cups after the last bite is swallowed. Don't try to tempt an Italian with an extra morsel after the espresso is served. (It's sort of the same as offering an American a cookie after they've brushed their teeth.) Also, coffee is never drunk *throughout* the meal in Italy because it too interferes with digestion—in an acidic way, rather than a curdling way—any Italian grandmother will tell you. However, the same *nonna* will also tell you that a shot of espresso at the end of the meal aids in digestion.

Juices, sodas, cocktails, and even sugarless ice tea all interfere with the flavor of the food. To savor the true taste of each ingredient is of utmost importance to Italians, as well as those who truly love Italian cooking. The only beverages that complement Italian cuisine are wine and water.

"But what about beer?" you might ask. Until recently, Italy did not have a rich beer tradition, but Peroni and Moretti have been around since the middle of the 1800's. Italians drink beer with pizza. This does not violate the Italian Food Rule: Wine or Water, Nothing Else, because pizza is not a meal. Pizza is...well...*pizza*. Neither wine nor water complement pizza as well as beer does. Kids and teenagers celebrate the lifting of the "no sodas" ban on pizza nights.

Then the next day it's back to wine or water, nothing else.

DID YOU KNOW?

It is bad luck to toast each other at the table with anything but wine.

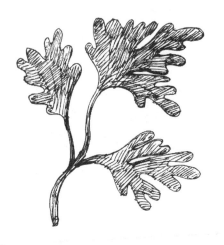

Rules For Drinking Wine

To Italians, wine and food go together. It is a marriage. Divorcing the two is next to impossible in Italy. You will never be invited to an Italian's home for drinks. You will not be offered a glass of wine after you take your coat off and before you sit down to eat, unless a full platter of appetizers makes its appearance first.

In a restaurant, you will not be asked what you want to drink before you order your meal. If the waiter offers you a glass of Prosecco before you order, you know two things: 1) the restaurant serves a lot of tourists; and 2) a complimentary appetizer will come with the spritzy white wine. If the bottle of wine you ordered with your meal arrives on the table before the food, the Italians at the table will not drink until at least the *antipasti* are served. They may not drink wine until they get to the main course.

A couple of years ago, a survey of over 800 American wine drinkers came up with the result that only 41 percent of the wine drunk was consumed while sitting down to a meal. Nineteen percent was consumed with appetizers and snack food (nuts, chips, etc.), and 14 percent was sipped in the kitchen while preparing food (so perhaps a taste of food, here or there). That means 26 percent of wine, consumed by Americans who profess to love the beverage, was drunk without food at all.

Perhaps Italians understand that the natural acidity of wine begs for food. It is assumed that the purpose of wine always is to accompany and enhance foods. And, more importantly, food enhances the flavor of wine. Where the tannins in wine dry out the mouth and impart a slightly bitter flavor, food stimulates the salivary glands and brings a more rounded taste to wine.

Italians are rarely pretentious about their wine choices or their wine/food pairing. The whole issue of choosing the "right" wine for a certain dish came from the fussy French and was copied by Americans who wished to show off their culinary acumen.

Italians tend to be regional in their wine selection. When in Rome, eating a Roman dish *Bucatini all'Amatriciana* or *Baccalà alla Trasteverina,* the wine selection will probably be a refreshing white from the Frascati wine-growing region on one of the "seven hills" just south of Rome. If the truffled dishes of Piemonte are served in Torino, a Barolo or Barbaresco, made from the local Nebbiolo grape, will be ordered. Although a Roman might on occasion order a Tuscan Chianti Classico, a Piemontese would never consider doing the same, unless he was dining in Siena. You will rarely see wines from France, Spain or the U.S. on an Italian wine list, unless you are in an ostentatious restaurant.

Vino della Casa, the house wine, will be local and, with very few exceptions, will taste great. It will complement the local food, but will not be a wine you would want to drink on its own. Italians don't. In regions where the local food does not go with white wine, such as Tuscany, you will rarely find a white house wine. In Venice, with its famous creamy *Baccalà Mantecato* and tapas-portioned *cicchetti*, the house wine will be a bubbly white Prosecco or cold Soave from the Veneto.

Glassware will range from small squat glasses used for both water and house wine, to standard generic stemmed glasses, great for most every Italian wine, to fine crystal stemware chosen to complement the aroma and taste of a fine Brunello. They all work for Italians. Again, they leave the pretentious glassware choices to the French and the Americans.

Most important—even though he was French—the Italians will agree with Andrè Simon (1877-1970), a wine merchant, gourmet, and prolific writer about wine, when he wrote, "Food without wine is a corpse; wine without food is a ghost; united and well matched they are as body and soul, living part-

"Super Tuscan" Is Not Italian

"Bring me one of those Super Tuscans, please," requests a tourist from San Francisco to the Roman waiter in an up-scale restaurant. "Something with cabernet sauvignon or merlot in it." The waiter will probably not be confused by the order of a Super Tuscan, but he will more likely bring the wine list than make a selection for his customer.

Although today the moniker "Super Tuscan" is universally used by Americans to denote a wide variety of fine red wines from Tuscany, the expression was originally adopted by English-language wine writers as an unofficial descriptor to describe high quality wines that had been classified by the Italian government as *vino da tavola* (table wine). The Italians have never used the term and there is no comparable phrase in the Italian language today.

No one really knows who coined the term "Super Tuscan," although many believe that the designation was first used by writer Burton Anderson, who covered Italy for *Wine Spectator* in the

1980s. This English term "Super Tuscan" came to stand for winemaking that dared to defy tradition and break the rules.

It is easy to imagine in 1971, Anderson was sipping a great glass of Tignanello, a cabernet sauvignon/cabernet franc/sangiovese blend, with its creator Marchese Piero Antinori, listening to the vintner complain about the fact that he couldn't get the Americans to pay the price the wine deserved. "It's all in the marketing," Anderson might have said. "You need a good catch phrase. How about 'Super Tuscan'?"

The term "Super Tuscan" describes any Tuscan red wine that does not adhere to traditional blending laws for the region. For example, Chianti Classico DOCG wines are made from a blend of grapes with Sangiovese as the dominant variety (at least 80 %) in the blend. If the winery doesn't follow the recipe, it doesn't get to use the designation.

Super Tuscans often contain grapes that were not traditionally grown in Italy, such as cabernet sauvignon, cabernet franc, merlot or syrah, making them ineligible for DOC(G) classification under the traditional rules.

In 1992, Italian authorities came up with a new category, *Indicazione Geografica Tipica* (IGT) that designates a geographic area, while giving wide latitude in winemaking. Many Super Tuscans today fall under this designation. While still a potent marketing device, the rubric "Super Tuscan" has become a sort of catchall for the pricier red wines of the region that don't follow the DOC(G) classifications.

If you want to discuss fine wine with an Italian, leave out the term "Super Tuscan" and start by using the IGT designation and then perhaps, talk about *vino particolare,* a good Italian term for an IGT wine that is particular, special or even, super.

DID YOU KNOW?

Although many Tuscan vintners wish the claim to fame of being the creator of the first Super Tuscan, most would agree that this credit belongs to Marchese Mario Incisa della Rocchetta and his wine Sassicaia, made from Cabernet Sauvignon at his Tenuta San Guido estate in Bolgheri. In 1950, he started making wine with French grapes using Italian methods. At its inception, Sassicaia was the family's personal wine. The 1968 vintage was released commercially after 1970 when the famous enologist, Giacomo Tachis, was brought on to make Sassicaia the full-bodied wine it is today.

The problem for these innovative vintners was that if they did not qualify for the DOC or DOCG designations, they were required to label their wine *Vino Rosso da Tavola* (Red Table Wine), a term usually applied low quality wines, and no one wanted to pay a high price for plain old red table wine, especially the Americans.

In the 1970s, Marchese Piero Antinori, whose

family had been making wine for more than 700 years, and was related to Marchese Incisa della Rocchetta, also decided to make a more complex wine that could tolerate aging by eliminating the then mandated white grapes from the Chianti blend, and instead added Bordeaux varietals (namely, Cabernet Sauvignon and Cabernet Franc). The resulting wine did not qualify for the Chianti Classico DOC. It was mere red table wine.

What was formerly Chianti Classico Riserva Vigneto Tignanello, denied the DOC designation as a Chianti Classico wine in 1971 because Antinori refused to use white grapes in the blend, became simply Tignanello (after the name of the vineyard), the second Super Tuscan, after its cousin Sassicaia.

NO BUTTER FOR THE BREAD

"Where's the butter for the bread?" asks a tourist from Chicago. "Can we get some butter out here?" asks a lady from Atlanta.

"*Perché?*" queries the waiter. *Perché?* indeed. In Italy, bread is not better with butter. Butter never meets bread on the Italian peninsula, except for a breakfast of a slice of toast with butter and *marmellata* or an after-school snack of bread, butter, and sugar or bread, butter and anchovies.

At lunch or dinner, Italians wouldn't think of spreading butter on the bread from the basket on the table. In fact, bread is served with the meal solely for the purpose of acting as the *scarpetta* - the little shoe. Italians say, "*fare la scarpetta*" to mean use as a little shoe of bread to scoop up the last remnants of sauce on the plate.

To ask for butter in a restaurant, or a family home, puts the host in a quandary. The kitchen may have a quarter kilo or more of butter, but it isn't table-worthy. There are no cute pats of butter or, even, butter dishes in restaurants or most homes.

When you visit Italy, give up bread and butter for the duration of your stay–you and your waistline will appreciate it–and think how good it will taste when you get home.

DID YOU KNOW?

Toasted bread slathered with butter and sprinkled with garlic salt is *not* Italian Garlic Bread. Make *fettunta* (known as *bruschetta* outside Tuscany)–slices of hot toasted Tuscan bread, rubbed with a clove of fresh garlic, splashed with fresh extra virgin olive oil and sprinkled with salt.

DANTE LOVED BREAD MADE WITHOUT SALT

Tourists are frequently surprised when they first taste traditional Tuscan bread that is always made without salt. Tuscans, especially Florentines, would not eat it any other way.

Dante agreed. *"Tu proverai sí come sa di sale lo pane altrui, e come è duro calle lo scendere e 'l salir per l'altrui scale."* In these lines from the *Paradiso* of "The Divine Comedy," Dante learns of his exile from Florence and is given some idea of the difficulties he will face. "You shall learn how salty is the taste of another's bread, and how hard a path the descending and the climbing another's stairs," he is told by Cacciaguida.

The Pisans get all the blame from some pundits for the bland bread made by the Florentines. Supposedly, they attempted to force Florence to surrender in one of their endless battles against each other by blockading the salt that arrived at the Pisan port, preventing it from reaching Florence via the Arno River.

Others claim that the widespread poverty in the Middle Ages is to blame when salt was too costly for the Tuscans to use in bread-making. (It's hard to credit this story because poor Italian peasants in other regions couldn't afford salt, but didn't give up making salted bread.)

I like to think it was the pope's fault. During the 14th to 16th centuries, it is said, the popes, who controlled much of the Italian peninsula (known as the Papal States), levied a tax on salt. Pope Paul III raised the tax in 1539 and the Perugians and the Tuscans refused to pay it. The government of Perugia even went to war over the issue—the Salt War of 1540. The Perugians lost the war, but some say the citizens then refused to buy the salt, thus forcing the *fornai* (bread bakeries) to produce salt-free bread. (Tuscan bread is one of the few that remains salt-free today, but there are many historical references to bread made without salt in other parts of Italy.)

During the 16th century in Tuscany, the Tuscan Medici dukes controlled all of the resources of the region, including salt. When they needed cash (for a war or for building a new villa) they raised the price on salt and other commodities. Thus, *pane toscano* (Tuscan bread) became bread famous throughout Italy for being *sciocco*, from the word in the Tuscan dialect for "insipid" (to Tuscans "*sciocco*" also means "stupid", but that doesn't fit this situation because they think salt-less bread is anything, but stupid). Those who are not Tuscan make fun of the bread of the region, but Tuscans, like Dante, mourn the loss of it when they travel.

Salt-less Tuscan bread is not intended for eating on its own. It's usually served along with the main meal and is meant for sopping up thick, rich, spicy sauces. The bread doesn't compete with the flavors in the dish; both are enhanced.

Tuscan bread has a rustic look with a crunchy crust. The soft middle part of the loaf is honey-combed in appearance. Its lack of salt helps keep it fresh for several days. Since it has no salt to hold in water, it does not form mold—it just becomes hard as a rock when it is stale—thus making it the basis of many of the tasty dishes that are renowned in Tuscan cuisine.

DID YOU KNOW?

The following Italian dishes are made with stale salt-free Tuscan bread:

Ribollita—a twice-boiled thick vegetable soup (*ribollita* means 're-boiled'), made of black and white cabbage, white beans and other vegetables, made thick with crumbled stale Tuscan bread or poured over toasted Tuscan bread.

Pappa al pomodoro—a bread-based thick tomato soup in which stale Tuscan bread is rehydrated and crumbled; then cooked with the tomatoes, basil and garlic to make a tasty *pappa.*

Panzanella–a summer salad dish. Stale Tuscan bread is soaked in water, squeezed into a damp mass, crumbled into a big salad bowl and cucumber, raw onion, fresh diced tomato and fresh basil leaves are added. The ingredients are tossed thoroughly with some extra virgin olive oil, salt and pepper.

Cacciucco–a fish chowder from Livorno made of fish, mollusks and crustaceans. The Livornese claim that the recipe should contain at least five types of fish to match the number of 'c's in the word *cacciucco*. Once cooked, the *cacciucco* is served on a bed of toasted Tuscan bread that has been rubbed with a clove of fresh garlic.

Fettunta/Bruschetta–"garlic toast" made with slices of hot toasted Tuscan bread, rubbed with a clove of fresh garlic, splashed with fresh extra virgin olive oil and sprinkled with salt. Don't try to cut into a completely stale loaf of Tuscan bread to make this; it's too hard to cut. Use slightly stale bread–too dry to eat untoasted, but perfect for *fettunta* or *bruschetta.*

LARD IS LUSCIOUS

Place a platter with a large rectangle of lard on the table, pass around a basket of warm toasted Tuscan bread slices, and you have a contented table of Italians. *Lardo di Colonnata* is delectable and has been an Italian traditional dish since before the time of Michelangelo.

Lardo is pork fatback and is 100% fat. Most Americans squirm at the idea of eating pure fat, and pig fat, at that. But olive oil is also 100% fat. Lard (*lardo*) is lower in saturated fat and cholesterol, and higher in mono- and poly-unsaturated fats than butter. Lard and butter aren't public enemy No. 1 anymore. Instead the hydrogenated fats–margarine, for instance, the so-called "healthy" fat of the 1970's–have turned out to be the "bad" fats.

For over one thousand years, *lardo* has been made in the same way in Colonnata, near Carrara. The marble quarrymen used to take a big slice of lard and a few dried tomatoes, wrapped in a hunk of bread, off to work each day. The high caloric sandwich would carry them through the long hours of hard labor.

The process for making *lardo* is complex. It starts in the fall when pigs of at least nine months of age and weighing over 350 pounds are butchered. Rectangular strips of fatback, each at least one and quarter inch thick, are cut. The maturation takes place in marble tubs (*le conche di marmo*) placed in caves or cool cellars. To give the lard its unique flavor the tubs are rubbed with garlic and the lard is immersed in brine. Sea salt mixed with spices and herbs (always rosemary, peppercorns, and garlic, but sometimes including anise seed, thyme, oregano, sage, nutmeg, and cloves) is rubbed over each slab in a thick layer. The strips are fit, puzzle-like, layer upon layer in the marble casks, repeating the process over and over. Once the tub is full, it is covered with a wooden lid or a marble cover. The curing time runs from a minimum of six months to one year.

Lardo di Colonnata is white with a pink streak. Thanks to the particular maturation procedure, the Lard of Colonnata is a natural product, free from preservatives and coloring. The best way to eat this lard is on toasted bread or on polenta, laying a paper-thin slice of room temperature *lardo* on the still warm bread or polenta. For a savory-sweet treat, dot sliced *lardo* with fig preserves or *mostarda di frutta* (an Italian condiment made with candied fruit and powdered mustard). Let the *lardo* melt on your tongue followed by the sweet taste with the mustard kick. Despite the amount of salt used in curing the fatback, *lardo* is surprisingly mild.

Next time the mixed appetizers (*crostini misti*) are passed, grab the small toast with the translucent fold of *lardo* melting on top before the Italians do. You will be in for a flavor treat.

DID YOU KNOW?

Despite its centuries-long history, the most eventful times for *lardo* have been recent. In April 1996, the powers-that-be realized that no *lardarium* had ever been inspected or authorized by the regional boards of health. European Union food inspectors got involved. Countless *conche di marmo* were sealed and several hundred pounds of lard were confiscated from Colonnata's dirt-floored cellars and caves. The resulting analysis revealed that all samples tested were found beyond reproach and it was proven once and for all that the use of marble containers posed no health threat.

Despite the laboratory findings, however, producers were ordered to meet existing health practices, including using preservatives and disposable plastic tubs, tiling the cellars, forbidding use of the caves for aging–essentially bankrupting the *lardarium* system.

The EU's action caused a grass-roots movement that led to *Lardo di Colonnata* becoming one of the first traditional Italian foods, made using many of the ancient methods, to be protected under the Arca del Gusto di Slow Food, supported by the Slow Food Italia organization, *Provincia di Massa Carrara* and the *Regione Toscana*. Twelve of the fourteen producers were able to remain in business.

To make sure they are getting traditionally made *lardo*, Italians ask to see the IGP (*Indicazione Geografica Protetta*) brand on the rind or the DOP (*Denominazione di Origine Protetta*).

Other regions produce tasty *lardo*, including:

1) *Lardo di Arnad*, once made in oak casks and now aged in steel containers, comes from Valle d'Aosta. It is sometimes stored thereafter in glass jars, covered with white wine.

2) From Cavour, a small town in the Piemonte region, a famous butcher, Silvio Brarda, produces a special rosemary-infused *lardo*, *Lardo al rosmarino di Cavour*.

3) Another Tuscan *lardo* is produced near Florence in the town of Greve. *Lardo Val di Greve*, made from special mature *Cinta Senese* pigs, is known for its reasonable price and delicate flavor.

PASTA IS NOT A SIDE DISH

For Italians pasta is a dish to be revered on its own, not shoved onto a plate beside some more important entrée.

Pasta is a *primo*–among the first dishes. It is to be served separately in its own bowl. The flavors of the pasta noodle and the accompanying sauce are to be savored without any other food–no bread, no vegetables, no meat or fish. Nothing should interfere with the enjoyment of a dish of pasta, properly sauced.

In fact, Italians will take care in telling you that it is "pasta with sauce" not "sauce with pasta". It is important that a light hand adds the sauce so that the flavor of the pasta noodle itself is not overwhelmed or covered up.

Once the pasta noodles are all gone, the small amount of remaining sauce can be captured and enjoyed by employing a small torn piece of bread, just big enough for one bite.

PASTA IS COOKED *AL DENTE*

In the '80s every want-to-be cook in America got a fresh pasta-making machine and at least once or twice made fresh pasta. The results were usually disappointing and the biggest problem was the resulting mushy, gummy pasta. There was frequently something wrong with the dough, but more often the fresh pasta was cooked much too long.

Italians know that the best pasta has some "chew" to it–pasta cooked *al dente* (literally "at the tooth"). Italians also know that it is next to impossible to achieve this texture with fresh pasta. The cooking time is usually about one to three minutes long and must be stopped somehow after the pasta is removed from boiling water.

Dried pasta is the answer. Americans seem to think that dried pasta is bad or old pasta (and frequently what Americans find on their grocery shelves fits those descriptions). Italians know that dried pasta, made by a reputable company, is flavorful and cooks up perfectly.

71

Dried pasta takes up to nine to eighteen minutes to cook properly, depending on the type of flour and the shape. The key is to get the center of the noodle to cook through (losing the telltale white spot and the tiny crunch when it is bitten) and then stop the cooking process immediately by removing the pasta from the boiling water, not just turning the heat off under the pot.

For some sauces it is best to take the pasta up to the last couple of minutes, drain it and then sauté it in the sauce for the final two minutes, thereby adding more flavor to the noodles.

Have you heard that old wives tale–throw the pasta against the wall–if it sticks, it's done? It's a sure fire way to make your kitchen wall a disgusting mess. The more pasta cooks, the gummier it gets, so if it sticks to the wall it's overdone. The only way to know if it's properly cooked is to bite it. It should be *al dente*, or firm to the bite, but not crunchy.

Did your favorite aunt rinse pasta after cooking and draining so it wouldn't stick together? This will make the pasta cold and rinse away the starch that helps bind the sauce to it. If it sticks together, it's overcooked. Or did she add olive oil to the cooking water to keep the pasta from sticking? Pasta shouldn't stick when properly cooked. If it's cooked with olive oil, the noodles will be coated and prevent the tasty sauce from sticking. The only ingredient to be added to the pasta water just as it starts to boil, before dropping in the dry noodles, is a small handful of large grain sea salt (or about 2 tablespoons of regular salt).

There are two cases where Italians demand fresh pasta. First, filled pastas, like *ravioli* or *tortellini*, where the filling must be fresh, not dried, must have fresh pasta to hold the filling inside. In this case, the cooking time is usually about three to five minutes and the pasta should still be *al dente*.

Second, fresh *tagliatelle*, usually bright yellow from the egg yokes in the pasta dough, is also a fresh-made pasta loved especially by northern Italians. It cooks up in two to three minutes (*al dente*, again) and calls for a delicate topping like butter and shaved white truffles. (For those on a budget, salt-free creamy butter and fresh cracked black pepper is almost as good.)

Italians will tell you that with food it isn't just the taste; it isn't just the look; it isn't just the aroma; it is also the texture that is important. Give your pasta some "chew."

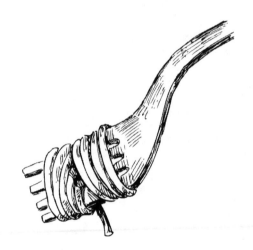

SPAGHETTI IS NOT SERVED WITH MEATBALLS

"Mamma mia, thatsa spicy meatball," the red-faced "Italian" man said each time his stereotypical wife plunked down a steaming plate of spaghetti and meatballs...until the antacid commercial hit its punchline. "Spaghetti and meatballs, now that's Italian!" is found in the script of many a B-movie. Even Lady and the Tramp have their first kiss over spaghetti and meatballs served up by Tony, the mustachioed Italian singing cook, in the 1955 movie.

The Italian Food Rule holds that there will be no meatballs on top of spaghetti. Spaghetti with meatballs is not an authentic Italian dish. (To find "spaghetti with meatballs" on a menu anywhere in Italy means that you are eating in a tourist trap.)

If you inquire about the dish in Italy, your waiter may laugh, but more likely sneer. If pasta and meatballs are served in the same meal, the two ingredients will be served separately–the spaghetti as a *primo* and the meatballs (*polpette*) as a *secondo*.

Spaghetti served with "red sauce" and topped with meatballs is an American creation. The pasta recipe probably made its first appearance in New York or New Jersey in the late 1800s, most likely as a reaction to the socio-economic conditions experienced by a wave of Italian immigrants who arrived at the turn of the 20th century. They left Italy poor and started lives in America poor. Meat was costly. For special occasions, when meat was served, the portions were small—too embarrassing to offer alone on the plate. But as a topping for cheap pasta and thin tomato sauce, meatballs the size of walnuts made the platter a celebration.

In the 1930s, the jolly Chef Boyardee was celebrated from coast to coast for his spaghetti with meatballs. Ettore Boiardi left Piacenza in 1915 at age 17 to land a job in the kitchen at the Plaza Hotel in NYC. By 1928, he had invented a meatball-making machine. Like Tony in the Lady and the Tramp, Ettore (soon known as Hector) liked the spicy meatballs and he put them in a can with spaghetti, ready to be opened at every American kid's lunch. No child in Italy will ever see spaghetti with meatballs for lunch or dinner.

Of course, with prosperity came exaggeration. The platter of pasta was the same size, but the sauce became thicker, drowning the spaghetti, and the meatballs grew to the size of a child's fist.

The Italian-American spaghetti and meatball

myth always invokes grandma's recipe. Marcella Hazan, the true expert on how Americans should prepare authentic Italian food, agreed with the Italian Food Rule. For those in search of the same flavor, she endorses a fine recipe for pasta with a meat sauce (*ragù*), but nixed untidy balls of meat that roll down a heap of over-cooked spaghetti.

DID YOU KNOW?

• Alfredo is a man's name not a pasta sauce–ask for pasta with a sauce containing *panna* (cream).

• Bolognese is a descriptive term–ask for *ragù alla Bolognese* for the rich meat sauce.

• You must pair the correct shape of pasta with the correct sauce–long pasta (*spaghetti*, *tagliatelle*) with tomato and smooth sauces and short pasta (*penne*, *rigatoni*) with chunky sauces.

• Pasta salads are not made with fresh pasta or long pasta or mayonnaise.

• Do not cut your spaghetti–twirl it on a fork against the edge of the bowl, unless you are less than ten years old, when you can use a spoon to help twirl the noodles.

• Pasta is never served with a sauce made with chicken or rabbit, but you might find a tasty *pappardelle sulla lepre* (wide pasta with wild hare sauce).

DON'T EAT BREAD WITH PASTA

Bread is not eaten with pasta in Italy. Bread accompanies the *secondo* (main dish), not the *primo piatto* (pasta course). The primary reason for this Italian Food Rule is that bread with pasta constitutes two starches being eaten together, each interfering with the taste of the other.

Many times bread is more of a utensil than a food. A small piece torn off a slice of bread–*scarpetta*–may be eaten after the pasta is finished to mop up those last traces of sauce that can't be caught by the fork.

Scarpetta means "little shoe" in Italian. *Fare la scarpetta*–do the little shoe–happens after every last pasta noodle has been eaten and traces of delicious sauce are still in the bowl. A person simply takes a piece of bread from the basket, tears off the appropriate sized piece, pinches an edge and scoops the sauce. That piece of bread transforms into a tiny shoe and the sauce is the slippery ground across which your little shoe is sliding, the sole picking up traces as it goes.

Tuscan bread, made with no salt, has little taste of its own so it is the perfect bread to *fare la scarpetta,* especially with spicy sauces.

Italians can be divided into two groups: those who do the *scarpetta,* and those few who don't. Some people do so only furtively because their mothers told them it was not good manners. More brazen food lovers just dig in with no regrets. A good *scarpettaro* will leave the plate with no trace of sauce.

DON'T EAT CHEESE WITH FISH

Nothing is more likely to raise the ire of your Italian waiter than to ask for some grated parmesan to go on your *spaghetti alle vongole* or *pasta al baccalà*. The reasons for the Food Rule are: logic, location, and tradition.

Except for salt cod (*baccalà*), canned tuna, cured sardines and anchovies (*acciughe*), Italians believe fish should be eaten fresh, close to the place and time that it is caught. Fish from the seas and rivers of Italy is mild tasting, delicate, and needs to be treated with a light touch when it comes to seasoning. The milky saltiness of cheese will overwhelm the flavor of the fish. And fishy cheese is just hard to contemplate, much less swallow.

Italian cheese producing regions tend to be inland and landlocked: parmesan in the north, pecorino in the hills of Tuscany, and buffalo mozzarella to the east and south of Naples. Famed for fish are the Ligurian, Sicilian, Adriatic and Tuscan coastal towns. Italians have been living the Slow Food, zero kilometer lifestyle for centuries. The recipes celebrate the location and availability of fresh ingredients: where there is fish there isn't cheese, and vice versa.

Location and tradition meet in the recipes passed down for generations. Italians don't move far from their places of birth and those places were city-states just 150 years ago. In Livorno, they argue over the types of shellfish and saltwater fish that should go into *cacciucco* (cheese never enters the discussion). In Bologna chefs add more cheese on top of a cheesy sauce covering ravioli stuffed with cheese, but not one thinks of filling his ravioli with fish. For centuries, tradition dictated that meat and dairy products were forbidden on Friday for religious reasons. Fish was the symbolic and nutritional replacement, but heaven forbade a topping of cheese.

Caveat: The wry Robert Trachtenberg, writing "Just Grate" in the *NY Times*, found the oldest surviving "Sicilian recipe–from around 400 B.C.–for fish: 'Gut. Discard the head, rinse, slice; add cheese and oil.'" Trachtenberg also browbeat famous chefs in Rome and Venice until they admitted to serving fish pastas with cheese added in the kitchen.

DID YOU KNOW?

• Cheese does not go with garlic and oil-based pasta sauces.

- Spicy cheeses (pecorino) go on spicy dishes.
- Don't add cheese–grated or cubed–to salads.
- Caprese (mozzarella, tomato, and basil) is not a salad; it's an *antipasto* or a *secondo*.
- Breaded meats and poultry do not get sprinkled with Parmesan cheese (chicken parmigiana or veal parmigiana are not Italian) or buried under a blanket of mozzarella.

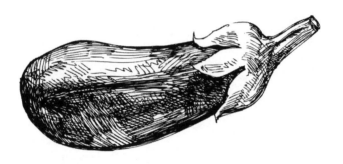

DON'T EAT EGGS IN THE MORNING

There is a reason that it is called an American Breakfast or an English Breakfast. If it contains eggs, it is not Italian. Italians are most likely to have a cappuccino and a pastry for the "most important meal of the day." They might stretch to a small bowl of yogurt and a half piece of fruit. But eggs are out.

In Italy, eggs are usually eaten hard-boiled, sliced in half (not crumbled) beside (not in) a lunchtime salad. Or, more commonly, they are prepared as a *frittata* (thin open-faced omelet) containing a few slices of artichoke, zucchini, eggplant or fried green tomatoes.

For dinner at home, Tuscans enjoy a savory dish of *uova al pomodoro* (eggs cooked in tomatoes) that consists of eggs sunny-side-up (one per person) cooked directly on a bed of chunky stewed fresh tomatoes, flavored with a bit of garlic, fresh basil and olive oil. Some crusty bread finishes the meal.

DID YOU KNOW?

- Orange juice is too acidic to drink in the morning.
- Bacon is *becon* or *pancetta affumicata* in Italy and is not seen at breakfast, but may be in *spaghetti alla carbonara.*
- Pancakes and waffles are loved by Italians, but are not Italian.
- Italians don't understand the concept of "breakfast for dinner."

A gift for you

Dear Bernard and Debra, In preparation for your fun BBC Food and Sightseeing tour in Italy, we thought you would enjoy this book. Enjoy your gift! Warmly, Barbara, Bela, and Cecilia

BISTECCA ALLA FIORENTINA IS
ALWAYS SERVED RARE

Bistecca alla Fiorentina (beefsteak Florentine style) must be served rare. Don't ask for it well done or, even, medium. It has very little fat marbling, so it gets tough when it is cooked too long.

This Tuscan steak is comparable to a T-Bone or porterhouse cut. It is the flavorful meat of the white, long-legged, grass-fed Chianina cattle.

The Chianina breed originate in the area of the Val di Chiana, are the tallest and heaviest breed in the world and one of the oldest, having been raised in Italy for at least 2000 years (the first written accounts appears in 55 AD).

Bistecca alla Fiorentina is never slathered with barbeque sauce, either during the grilling or after. Typically weighing in at one kilo (2.2 pounds), the steaks are grilled over a charcoal fire (5 minutes on each side and 15 minutes standing on end on the bone), and then seasoned with salt, black pepper, and perhaps, a splash (after the steak is removed from the fire) of olive oil. *Bistecca* is frequently garnished with a lemon wedge. It's okay to share one steak for two. Don't ask for steak sauce or a pat of butter.

If cooked properly, *Bistecca alla Fiorentina* will be tender enough to cut with a table knife. If it's cooked too long it will be as tough as shoe leather. If your chef agrees to cook a Chianina beefsteak to medium or well done, he isn't Italian or you are eating in a tourist trap.

DON'T PASS THE GRAVY

Gravy–all those meaty drippings, fats, flour and other thickeners, and, perhaps, a hunk of butter– what's not to like? It's good on everything from meat, poultry (especially turkey), mashed or stir-fried potatoes, cornbread, grits, to good old buttermilk biscuits. Gravy ties the meal together. Sometimes, gravy is the main ingredient of a meal.

For Italians, that's just the problem. In Italy, different dishes are meant to be on...well...*different* dishes. In other words, the potatoes, either mashed or oven-roasted, are served on a separate plate than the *ossobuco*. Each food, made with its own special recipe, is meant to be savored separately, so that you can taste each ingredient the cook used.

The *ossobuco* may have some pan drippings around it, but those savory drips are not to touch the sweet spring peas that have been steamed with only a couple of whole cloves (not crushed) of garlic and a sprig or two of parsley. The peas, a *contorno* (side dish), are to be served to you on a separate plate. You are to eat them from that plate and not transfer them to your *secondo* (the main dish, the *ossobuco*) to let them roll them around in the meat sauce.

Gravy, by its very nature, is meant to tie diverse foods together in a, hopefully, harmonious taste. Italian menus are created with care so that the pairing of the dishes is harmonious without having to be bound together by a saucy tsunami of gravy.

TRIPE IS TASTY TO TUSCANS

Tripe (*trippa*) is what Americans coyly refer to as "variety meats" and what some Italian aficionados sometimes call the *quinto quarto* (fifth quarter) of the animal. Usually it refers to the lining of one of the four chambers of a ruminant's stomach, usually a young ox. But a *trippaio* (tripe butcher) will sell the bits and pieces of the *quinto quarto* of veal, beef, and pork. Italians, especially Florentines, swear that *trippa* is one of the Italian delicacies that doesn't get enough attention.

When properly cooked, Italians claim these meats are delicious–tender, mild yet flavorful, without being overtly fatty.

Trippa alla fiorentina is the white honey comb muscle of the cow's second stomach cooked in a rich tomato sauce, but the classic is the *panino col lampredotto*–long-simmered, light purple-brown from the cow's fourth stomach served as a sandwich at lunchtime with either a *salsa piccante* (hot chili flakes and olive oil) and/or a *salsa verde* (parsley, capers, garlic and anchovies, among other ingredients)–it's called *completo* when you want both sauces–at one of the specialist *trippaio* carts parked on sidewalks and in piazzas. (Florence boasts of nine tripe stands, one for each neighborhood in the historic center of the city, and 23 more in the periphery of the city.)

The true skill, learned young, is how to eat this soggy sandwich (*panino col lampredotto*), with its saucy meat and bread that has been quickly dunked in the meat juice, without getting it on your shirt or tie. The "lampredotto lean" (kind of like the Tower of Pisa) creates the right angle, but you still need plenty of napkins to wipe your chin.

For a change, an Italian might ask for *poppa* (udder–cooked for nearly eight hours to melting tenderness) on toasted bread or *nervetti* (tendons–more texture than flavor) cooked in tomato sauce. In Rome, intestines from milk-fed calf or lamb are used to make *pajata*. In Sicily the same are grilled and sold on the streets–*stigghiole* is what you need to ask for if you want to try them.

The home cook will stop by a favorite *trippaio* in the market and find creamy white or russet mats of raw tripe from all four chambers of the cow's stomach, dominating the glassed-in counter, accompanied by ears, hoofs, cheeks, muzzles, testicles, udders, kidneys and other internal and external body parts of pork, veal and beef. Although you will probably not be served tripe as a dinner guest in an Italian home, the number of *trippai* doing good business in the Italian food markets show that tripe is being dished out at many an Italian family lunch table.

Try a *mezza porzione* (half portion) at your favorite trattoria next time you want to be Italian for a day.

THEY EAT HORSES, DON'T THEY?

In Europe and Japan, it is a staple, and in Sweden horse meat outsells mutton and lamb combined. Residents of Austria, Belgium, Canada, Chile, China, France, Germany, Iceland, Indonesia, Kazakhstan, Malta, Mongolia, the Netherlands, Norway, Poland, Slovenia, and Switzerland all consume horse meat. But Italy surpasses all other countries in the European Union in horse meat consumption.

The meat itself is similar to beef, although many say it is slightly sweeter in taste (somewhere between beef and venison) and has a less complex flavor. That said, many Italians argue that it is a healthier option than beef, being both lower in fat and having a higher content of protein, iron, Omega-3, Vitamin B-12 and glycogen.

It is an inexpensive meat and it used to be the red meat for the poor, but now is consumed by all economic classes. One reason for the increased consumption came about 10 years ago with the fears of BSE (mad cow disease) in beef. The disease is not found in horses.

Don't worry if you are afraid that you might not recognize the difference between horse and beef in the market. In 1928, Italian legislation was passed to prohibit the sale of horse meat together with other meats in the same stores. In the big food markets, horse meat is sold at a specialty stand by specialist horse butchers. The Roman Catholic Church prohibited eating horse meat in the 8th century, and the taboo still remains, but is not followed by many Catholic Italians. On a menu, keep an eye out for the words *cavallo* or *carne equina*, and in Sardinia the dialect word for horse is *cuaddu*.

Horse meat is used in a variety of Italian recipes: as a stew called *pastissada* (typical of Verona), served as steaks, as *carpaccio* (raw), or made into *bresaola* (cured). Even classic Italian *mortadella* sausage can be had in a horse meat variety. Minute shredded strips of salted, dried and smoked horse meat called *sfilacci* are popular in the Veneto region. A long-cooked stew called *pezzetti di cavallo* combines cubed horse meat with tomato sauce, onions, carrots and celery. Horse meat sausages (*salsiccia di equino*) and salamis are traditional in northern Italy. In Sardinia, *sa petza 'e cuaddu* is one of the most popular meats and sometimes is sold in typical kiosks with bread. Donkey is also cooked, for example as a stew called *stracotto d'asino* and as meat for sausages e.g. *mortadella d'asino*. The cuisine of Parma features a horsemeat tartare, called *pesto di cavallo*, marinated in lemon juice with fresh garlic and chopped parsley.

Visitors to the north and south of Italy will have many chances to try horse meat, if they are so inclined. It's a regional Italian food that a tradition going back centuries.

DID YOU KNOW?

Today, in Tuscany, consumption of horse meat is rare, although there is one stand, Pica Nicolino Elena, in the *Mercato Centrale* of Florence where specialty horse butcher Nicola Ricci has sold a wide variety of products for decades, as did his father before him. There used to be five stands in the market selling horse meat. Florence has a couple of restaurants that offers a horse steak and Da Giulio, a trattoria in Lucca, regularly has a popular dish of marinated raw *cavallo alla tartara* on the menu.

BACCALÀ BINDS AND DIVIDES ITALY

In the U.S. you can count on finding a burger at every truck stop, small town or major city. In the U.K. the same could be said about fish and chips. In Italy, it's *baccalà* (salt cod). In the case of hamburgers or fish and chips, the recipe never varies much, but the recipe for salt cod changes drastically from region to region in Italy. Don't ask for *baccalà alla Livornese* in Venice or *baccalà mantecato* in Puglia.

It's not hard to imagine why salt cod became the go-to food around the Italian boot. In times before trucks and refrigeration, the transport of fresh fish was impossible. Despite this fact, the Roman Catholic Church mandated days of abstinence when meat could not be eaten. Salted or dried fish became a Friday and Lenten favorite. It had the added benefit of being very inexpensive and was a protein staple for the poor. Cod boasts remarkable nutritional properties: it contains over 18% protein, which once dried rises to almost 80%.

There are two forms of dried codfish–

stockfish and salt cod. Stockfish or *stoccafisso* is made using the smaller cod, dried on sticks in the cold dry air of Scandinavia, creating a very light, easily transported stick fish, thus the name. Salt cod or *baccalà* is created from cod, three to six feet long, split, and salted on wood planks for about ten days, thus only partially drying them. Today, Italy's *baccalà* and *stoccafisso* all come from Norway.

Salt cod has many of the characteristics of fresh cod: large, soft flakes of succulent, opaque flesh with slightly chewy firm texture from the salting, and not at all fishy in flavor. To prepare it, the cook rinses the salt off it and soaks it in cold water for 12 or more hours, depending upon its thickness, changing the water 2-3 times daily. (Stockfish takes a couple of extra days to rehydrate.) Once it has soaked it is skinned, deboned, and ready to be made into the local recipe.

In Veneto, *baccalà* is considered a real delicacy: *Baccalà alla Vicentina* (slowly braised with onions, anchovies and milk) and *Baccalà Mantecato* (a mashed and whipped preparation with extra virgin olive oil, lemon and parsley) are always served with white polenta. Some other popular recipes are *Baccalà alla Livornese* (with tomatoes, garlic, parsley and basil), cooked throughout Tuscany; *Baccalà Fritto* (salt cod chunks fried in a simple egg and flour batter) and *Baccalà all'Agrodolce* (with tomatoes, cooked in wine, flavored with red pepper, pine nuts and sultana raisins), which are both found in Rome. *Baccalà alla*

100

Pizzaiola (salt cod covered with tomatoes, bread-crumbs, capers, plenty of oregano and baked in the oven) and *Baccalà alla Napoletana* (the *baccalà* is fried and then placed in a simmering tomato sauce, with olives, capers and pine nuts) are recipes from Naples. The Neapolitans, even today, boast of the highest consumption of both stockfish and dried salted cod. They claim there are 365 different ways to eat *baccalà*–one for every day of the year.

As you travel around Italy, ask for *baccalà* at least once at each stop to taste the true regionalism of the country.

DID YOU KNOW?

Salt cod came to the ports of Livorno, Genoa and Naples in the 11th century, brought by Basque sailors, who ventured into the waters of the northern Atlantic, hunting the whales that passed through the Bay of Biscay. They came into contact with the Viking sailors, who dried the fresh-caught cod in the cold dry North Sea winds and then broke it into pieces and chewed it like a biscuit. In the 13th century, the Portuguese, realizing the commercial value of the easily-stored dried fish, cornered the market, sending their ships as far as Greenland. They added salt to dry the fish faster, giving rise to *bacalhau* (derived from the Latin, meaning "*baculus*" or stick). They traded salt cod along the western coast of the Italian peninsula.

The history of baccalà in Venice only dates back to 1431 when a Venetian ship, laden with spices and 800 barrels of Malvasia wine, departed from the island of Crete under the command of the sea captain Piero Querini, and headed for the North Sea and Flanders. When the ship reached the English Channel, the route was disrupted by a violent storm that, after breaking the rudder, blew the ship north for many days. Boarding lifeboats, the crew (only 14 of 68 survived) landed on the uninhabited rock of Sandoy, in Norway's northern Lofoten Islands.

For four months, the Venetians lived with the Norwegian fishermen, and learnt the art of preserving cod. Norway's unique climatic conditions of low temperatures, dry air and a low amount of precipitation were (and still are) perfect for air-drying cod in open tents. Cod preserved in this way can last for years.

Captain Querini returned home with sixty dried stockfish. He told the ruling Doges how the Norwegians dried the fish in the wind until it became as hard and then they beat it and spiced it turning it into a soft and tasty mix. The recipe was known by the Spanish words *baccalà mantecato* (creamed codfish). Querini went back to Norway many times, becoming a major trader in dried and salted codfish.

DON'T USE BOTTLED ITALIAN SALAD DRESSING

To dress a salad in Italy is simplicity itself: bring a bowl of salad greens (preferably one to three varieties of radicchio tossed together–that's all) to the table, add a generous splash of the best extra-virgin olive oil available, a small spray of red-wine vinegar or lemon juice, a substantial sprinkle of salt and a bit of fresh ground black pepper; toss again and serve on a salad plate (don't infect the leafy greens with leftover pasta sauce or juice from the *ossobuco* by reusing those plates).

Note that the ingredients are added to the salad greens sequentially, not shaken into a vinaigrette. The French invented vinaigrette.

Once you master the way to dress an Italian salad, the only debate left is whether inexpensive balsamic vinegar (not the costly traditional DOP ambrosia from Modena) is an acceptable substitute for red-wine vinegar. Purists would say emphatically, "No", but the number of Florentine neighborhood restaurants that bring the sweeter version of vinegar to the table seems to argue for, at least, an acceptable option to the Food Rule.

Italian Dressing, known and loved in the United States (as well as Canada, the U.K. and most of the British colonies), is a vinaigrette-type salad dressing, consisting of water, vinegar or lemon juice, vegetable oil, chopped bell peppers, usually sugar or high fructose corn syrup, and various herbs and spices including oregano, fennel, dill, dried oleoresin paprika and salt. Onion and garlic are often added to intensify the dressing's flavor. Usually it is bought bottled (containing also xanthan gum, calcium disodium edta, and sulfiting agents) or prepared by mixing oil and vinegar with a packaged flavoring mix consisting of dehydrated vegetables and herbs.

North American-style Italian dressing, especially Creamy Italian, which consists of the same ingredients, with buttermilk or mayonnaise added to make it creamy, is not acceptable to the Italian palate. (*"Che schifo"* or *"Che esagerazione!"* say Italians.) Don't ask for it in a restaurant in Italy or, particularly, from the cook in an Italian home.

Italian Dressing is not sold in Italy. Needless to say, you will also not find the following dressings in any Italian kitchen: Thousand Island, Ranch, Blue Cheese, Russian, Louis, Honey Dijon, French, Ginger Honey, and, perhaps surprisingly, Caesar Salad Dressing.

Try being Italian for a while–leave the salad dressing bottles in the fridge and simply add a bit of extra virgin olive oil, red wine vinegar, salt and pepper to some fresh leafy salad greens. You will be surprised by what you taste for the very first time.

DID YOU KNOW?

Caesar Dressing is much more American than Italian. It is reported that Caesar Cardini created the salad and the dressing in Mexico. Caesar (born Cesare) came from near Lago Maggiore in northern Italy. He and his brother Alex emigrated to the U.S. after World War I. The Cardini family lived in San Diego, but operated a restaurant in Tijuana to circumvent Prohibition. Supposedly, on July 4th in 1924, the salad was created on a busy holiday weekend at Caesar's Restaurant. Caesar was short of supplies, so he concocted this salad with what was on hand: romaine lettuce and croutons dressed with parmesan cheese, lemon juice, olive oil, egg, garlic, black pepper, and Worcestershire sauce. A bit of a showman, he prepared it at the table. This was the only thing truly Italian about Caesar Salad–a salad should be dressed at the table or right before it comes to the table.

DON'T DIP BISCOTTI IN COFFEE

Italians are very particular about what they dip their biscotti into. Pretty much it is a list of one–Vin Santo.

The subtly sweet, crisp almond cookies are loved throughout the world, but have their origin in Italy. The word "biscotti" is the plural form of *biscotto*, which originates from the ancient Latin word *biscoctus*, meaning "twice-baked." By baking them twice, biscotti (known in Tuscany as *cantucci* or *cantuccini*) lose any excess moisture, which ensures a crisp, dry cookie perfect for dipping. In Vin Santo. Only.

Vin Santo or *vino santo* (holy wine) is a style of Italian dessert wine. Traditional in Tuscany, these sweet high alcohol, late harvest wines are made from white grape varieties such as Trebbiano and Malvasia, which are hung to dry before pressing to increase their sugar content. The most likely origin of the name Vin Santo was the wine's historic use in religious Mass, where sweet wine was often preferred. Some of the earliest references to a "*vinsanto*" wine come from the Renaissance era sales logs of Florentine wine merchants.

So if, after dinner, you start reaching for the biscotti on the plate in the middle of the table to dip into your coffee, stop and think of the number of Italian Food Rules you are about to break–eating after coffee, putting crumbs in coffee, and perhaps, drinking cappuccino after 10am.

First, Italians consider coffee as both a palate cleanser and a *digestivo*. Biscotti and Vin Santo are dessert (*dolce*) and made for each other. Traditional biscotti eaten alone will put your teeth in peril. Dunking them in Vin Santo is the perfect solution. The best sip is the last containing all of the delicious biscotti crumbs.

That's Amaro – Italy Loves It's Digestivos

The smoothly running digestive system is crucial to an Italian's health and happiness. This concern is the basis of so many of the Italian Food Rules. You already know that you do not put uncooked milk on a full stomach (*cappuccino*, *caffellatte*, *gelato*); you do not eat "cold" melon without the "heat" of prosciutto or salt or *peperoncino*; you do not eat leftovers; and you do not overeat. Having eaten *well*, however, an Italian may partake of an herbal digestive drink after dinner.

The first attempts to aid digestion using aromatic herbs and seeds steeped in liquids were made by the Greeks and Romans. Yet today, no country can match Italy for the sheer variety of digestive remedies available. They traveled from the pharmacies of the 1800s, intended as palliatives to counter all sorts of ailments and physical imbalances, to restaurants, bars and the dinner table in the 20th century. They are bitter–that's *amaro*.

These homemade restoratives, generally bitter herbs, plants and other botanicals blended into an alcohol base, live on commercially today in the form of digestives. Digestives are not the usual after-dinner drinks, like brandies, grappas and other distilled products that are meant to add a pleasant intoxicating after-note to a meal, or the sweet high-alcohol wines, like Vin Santo, which give you a final sweet taste, but not the fullness of a three-layer cake.

These digestives, or *digestivi*, are known collectively as *amari*. The word refers to the bitterness that unifies this disparate group of liqueurs. Dozens of *amari* are produced in Italy. Each has a proprietary formula made by distilling a wide variety of herbs and spices and tempered in barrels or bottles. *Amari* have been toted in Italy to cure overeating, flatulence, hangovers, gas pains, cramps of all kinds, baby colic and cholera. One theory is that bitterness, typically associated with poison, cues the body to accelerate the production of saliva and digestive juices.

No one *amaro* shares the same makeup or ingredients with another. For example: Amaro Averna from Sicily is comprised of citrus, herbs, roots, and caramel; Cynar is an *amaro* made from 13 herbs and artichokes (*Cynara scolymus*), from which the drink derives its name; Nocino, is a *digestivo* made from green walnuts; Unicum, formerly a Hungarian *amaro*, contains 40 herbs and is aged in oak casks

110

(the Zwak family, holder of the secret Unicum recipe, emigrated to Italy after WWII); Vecchio Amaro del Capo, a herbal and minty *amaro* is made in Calabria; and Fernet-Branca, probably the most world-famous *amaro*, is made from a secret recipe of 27 herbs obtained from five continents.

Don't succumb to the distasteful practice of doing Fernet-Branca shots at your local bar in Los Angeles or New York in an effort to be cool. Sip a small glass after a four-course dinner at you favorite restaurant in Turin or Milan.

DID YOU KNOW?

Fernet-Branca was created by a self-taught herbalist in Milan in 1845. The secret recipe for this *digestivo*, first sold in pharmacies, includes aloe from South Africa, rhubarb from China, gentian from France, galangal from India or Sri Lanka, chamomile from Italy and Argentina, saffron, red cinchona bark, myrrh from Madagascar (yes, that's right—myrrh), and elderflower. The brew is aged in oak barrels for twelve months. It is about 40% alcohol. Fernet Branca is considered by some as a perfect cure for a hangover, but Italians drink it as a *digestivo* after a long meal.

Nocino is an *amaro* that can be found in most restaurants and ordered as a *digestivo*. But it is also the most popular *amaro* for the home-made *digestivo*, probably because of the ease of its recipe. Its main ingredient is green walnuts picked long before they are ready to eat.

The regions of Campania and Emilia-Romagna are the biggest producer of walnuts in Italy. Traditionally, the walnuts are picked by a woman (there is a bit of the pagan about this concoction) on the eve of June 24th, the *Festa di San Giovanni* (St. John the Baptist's saint day), the recipe is made the next day, after the *noci* have rested overnight, and then the brew is put away until *Ognissanti* (All Saints Day), November 1st, when it is drunk to honor the dead. Thereafter, it is sipped as a *digestivo* after the big December holiday meals.

To make Nocino, the walnuts (*noci*) are cleaned and quartered, put into round glass bottles with a mixture of alcohol, sugar, cinnamon, and cloves and allowed to rest in a warm sunny place. The liquid seeps into the nuts and turns dark brown. More sugar and spices are added and, if the liquid has become too strong, a little water is added.

Pellegrino Artusi (1820-1911), the father of modern Italian cooking, reportedly suffered from a "delicate stomach" and noted in his seminal cookbook that the digestive and tonic powers of this dark and sweet liqueur were the perfect end to those heavier meals later on in the year when the cooler months arrive. Artusi's Nocino contained unripe walnuts, alcohol (95%), white sugar, ground cinnamon, whole cloves, water, and the rind of one lemon. Sealed tightly in a large glass vessel, stored in a warm place, shaken "every now and then", the concoction was ready in forty days or so. A couple of days before November 1st he would have a little taste. If it was too "*spiritoso*" (too high in alcohol), Artusi advised adding a cup of water or two. Then, when the liqueur is ready, strain it first through a cloth, and then to clarify it, again through a finer cloth or paper, such as a modern coffee filter, before bottling.

Artusi also recommended an *amaro* he called "Cinchona Elixir" made with "bruised Peruvian cinchona bark" and "bruised dried bitter orange peel."

DON'T ASK FOR A DOGGY BAG

The Italian Food Rule: Don't Ask for a Doggy Bag, has strange antecedents because, according to some, the doggy bag's first appearance was in the 6th century BC…in Rome. Apparently, when invited to a banquet at the neighbor's villa the ancient Roman would bring a napkin or two. It was a compliment to the host to take some of the dinner home wrapped up in your napkin. But perhaps with the fall of the empire the custom fell into disfavor. During the Middle Ages, the leftovers went first to the kitchen staff, then to the lower order of servants, and then out the backdoor to the beggars in the courtyard.

In modern times, there seem to be three reasons that Italians don't ask for a take-out container. (The term doggy bag or doggie bag is an Americanism that entered the European lexicon mostly to complain about the practice.)

First, Italian food is made to order, to be eaten as the chef envisioned it, immediately as the dish arrives on the table. It is not to be eaten at another temperature (cold pizza), in another form (*bistecca alla fiorentina* sliced in a sandwich), or mixed together (*pasta alla carbonara* with a chunk off a veal chop resting on top).

Second, servings in Italian restaurants tend to be of the appropriate size so that the diner does not get too full by eating everything on the plate. A light eater does not order an *antipasto*, a *primo*, a *secondo*, and a *dolce*–one or two courses are enough.

Third, Italians look at food left on the plate as scraps, not leftovers. There's a difference. It's not good manners to ask to take home kitchen scraps.

I learned about this Italian Food Rule years ago, when I was a regular at La Maremma on Via Verdi in Florence. One evening, I ordered my favorite pasta and then saw ostrich (*filetto di struzzo con salsa di vino rosso*) on the menu. The owner, Enzo Ragazzini, explained that the ostrich was grown in Italy and urged me to try "*un piatto speciale e buono.*" I agreed, forgetting to ask for a half-portion of the pasta. After some shared *crostini*, my large plate of *penne con funghi e tartufi* arrived, steaming, fragrant, and oh so scrumptious. I just had to eat the whole thing.

Almost full, my eyes popped wide when a beautifully presented filet of ostrich–round, about two inches high and four inches in diameter, like a classic filet mignon at a good steakhouse in the U.S.–with a deep purple-brown wine sauce and a sprig of fresh rosemary, was placed in front of me.

The *filetto* was perfect, pink, tender, complemented in every way by the accompanying sauce. But it was huge. I could not do it justice in one sitting. Not after that pasta (and *crostini* and wine). I could have shared it with my friends, but as luck would have it I was eating with two vegetarians.

I couldn't let half a filet of ostrich, my first ostrich dish, go to waste. And I did not want the chef to get the wrong idea—I loved every bite. So I asked Enzo in my almost non-existent Italian, if there was any way he could wrap the half filet up so I could take it back to my apartment. This conversation took a while. He even resorted to some English to clarify my desire. After I finally came up with "*da portare via, per favore*," a phrase more suited to a pastry shop than a restaurant, he left with the plate, shaking his head.

He returned in a bit and showed me a small used, but clean, plastic bag with a warm aluminum-wrapped half filet of ostrich. I reach for it to put it quickly in my shopping satchel, out of sight. He wouldn't let it go. He sat down at the table and in a mix of Italian and English proceeded to give me the recipe (did I mention that I do not cook?) for the red wine sauce that graced the filet on the original plate. He could not envision it being served any other way.

He could not imagine that I would slice this tender filet of ostrich up with a little mustard and

117

mayo in a *panino*, or toss it into a microwave oven to warm it up to go on a plate beside a similarly zapped potato (my kind of cooking). No, I was instructed on how to make the exact same wine sauce as the chef. I took notes.

DID YOU KNOW?

In Rome the Italian Food Rule: Don't Ask for a Doggy Bag is starting to crumble. Some say that Michelle Obama is to blame. In 2009, Michelle was in Rome during the G8 Conference. Michelle, together with her two daughters, dined at a restaurant near the Pantheon. The family ordered three pasta dishes–*carbonara*, *amatriciana* and *bolognese*–but the meal turned out to be too hearty for the three Obama girls. Michelle asked the waiter to pack the leftovers into a bag to take home. According to the news reports, the First Lady's effort to make sure the food did not go to waste was widely understood as a public encouragement to save more and waste less.

By 2010, a non-profit group that works with homeless people in Milan, *Cena dell'Amicizia,* began a project called "*Il buono che avanza,*" ("the good that advances" or "the good things left over"). Restaurants in the Milan area can voluntarily take part, whereupon they are provided with doggy bags and an "*Il buono che avanza*" sticker created by the non-profit organization. "The idea is to fight the idea of a throw-away, consumerist society where waste is normal and recycling (even of food) is looked down upon," claimed *Cena dell'Amicizia.*

From all appearances, Florence, Tuscany and most of the rest of Italy will hold tight to the Italian Food Rule: Don't Ask for a Doggy Bag. Leftovers do not constitute food in a country that prides itself in a cuisine that has not seen change in centuries and is not ready for reheating in the modern microwave oven.

TAKE-AWAY PIZZA RULES

Before the turn of the millennium, pizza delivery was rare. In fact, prepared food delivery is almost unheard of in Italy because food is meant to be eaten hot, not tepid and not reheated, with fresh ingredients, tasting exactly as the cook envisioned the dish. This is especially important for pizza, which now can be delivered in most mid-sized to large cities by a guy on a Vespa, or picked up at the corner pizzeria and taken back to your hotel room.

Eating pizza in Italy is supposed to be a social event to be enjoyed with friends in a festive setting. Not on the kitchen table, half-warm, out of a cardboard box.

Pizza is never, never, never to be eaten as a leftover, cold or nuked, while standing in your kitchen.

Pizza made by a *pizzaiolo* in a wood-burning pizza oven (the only pizza worth eating) is a delicate thing. The crust is thin, the sauce is fine and fresh, and the other ingredients are newly sliced and few.

121

Within minutes after it is slid via a special paddle (the loading peel) from the fiery maw of the oven, it must be eaten immediately or it will be only a figment of its former gloriousness.

Leftover pizza is table scrap–literally, it is meant to be thrown away in the nearest bin–not to be put in a box, congealed mozzarella and mushroom bits, and all, to be carried home or to your hotel minibar fridge.

Treat pizza with the respect it (and the *pizzaiolo*) deserves and eat it hot and fast in a noisy pizzeria with friends. It's worth that first-bite blister on your palate. Better that you remember that pain the next day, rather than noshing on the soggy remnants of a once savory slice.

KISS THAT PANINO

Keep It Simple Stupid (KISS) is what an Italian would say looking at the sandwiches Americans love to eat. Now that "*panini*" are all the rage in the U.S. makes the overloaded sandwiches all the more egregious. A *panino* is *pane* (bread) with an *–ino* suffix to denote a small roll. Inside the small roll (not sliced bread) should be one or two slices of one or two, possibly three, ingredients. The idea is to be able to *taste* each ingredient, not to have them become some indecipherable jumble of flavors.

A foot-long sandwich with ten different spreads, cheeses, meats and lettuces is not Italian. The term *panino* as used in the U.S. usually means a sandwich that is heated under a *panino* press. The machine might have been invented in Italy, but not all *panini* are heated. Most are not because, again, the idea is to taste each ingredient. Also, butter never enters the equation–you will never find a buttered, toasted sandwich in Italy.

Venice is famed for its sliced bread (without a

crust) enclosing one to three ingredients and mayonnaise (mayo is not found in *panini* in other regions). These are not *panini*, but are Venetian *tramezzini*, which like all other regional specialties, should only be eaten in Venice, where they know how to make them.

If you see large sandwiches in glassed cases of coffee bars and self-serve eateries in the popular tourist towns of Florence, Rome and Venice, be aware that they are probably stale, are not traditional *panini* and are eaten only by foreigners. If you see Italians lining up at a window of a tiny shop where small warm, soft rolls of white bread are being torn open and filled with a thin slice of folded *mortadella* (no mayonnaise or mustard) or perhaps, a smear of goat cheese and a couple of slices of a spicy *salame*, get in line and have the best *panino* of your life.

DON'T EAT WHILE WALKING

Italians never eat or drink while they're walking. They have no culture of snacking on the types of food that Americans are frequently noshing on as they hurry from place to place–no Big Gulps, bags of Cool Ranch Doritos, Big Macs, or even, a *panino con la mortadella* (bologna sandwich). (Yes, sadly there are Big Macs in Italy, but they are being eaten–slowly–while at the table provided, not on the run.) There are no take-away sippy cups for coffee or cappuccino in Italy.

This aversion to eating and drinking while walking is learned at a young age. It's taught by a mother who values spotless clothes on her offspring and wants her family at the table on time and hungry, not stuffed with chips or a giant soda before the meal even begins. Italians stay thin by eating three meals a day at a table, not grazing on their feet, on the run.

So what about *gelato*? Yes, it is an exception to the rule. Italians walk while licking a small (2.50 €

125

or less) cone—a cone, not a cup—of *gelato*. If you are eating gelato out of a cup, you should be sitting in the *gelateria* or on a nearby bench. If you order a large cone (more than 2 scoops) you are not Italian.

While Americans are eating on the run to the next meeting, the Italians are sitting at a table, taking small mouthfuls, resting their cutlery between bites, discussing the food—because it is worthy of discussion. In case you were wondering, Italians do not eat in the car, either.

ITALIANS DON'T SNACK

There are Pringles, corn chips, candy, chewing gum, Cokes (not Pepsi), canned sweetened ice tea, Tic-Tacs, M&Ms and Mars Bars in any coffee bar or small grocery store in Italy. But who buys these snacks? Tourists…mostly.

Traditionally, Italians don't snack…with a couple of exceptions. First, at around 11am, Italians will stop by the local bar for an espresso. Between 4pm and 6pm and between 11pm and midnight, they will visit the gelateria for a small (maximum two scoops) cone. In the winter, the afternoon espresso may be changed out for a hot chocolate (*cioccolato caldo*) and the gelato may be forsaken for a hot fresh-made *bombolone* (fried doughnut). Also, in the winter a small bag of hot roasted chestnuts may become an early evening snack before dinner.

The name for these snacks is *merenda*, derived from the Latin "*mereo*", which means "that which you should deserve"–a well-deserved snack.

In Venice, the afternoon *merenda* is sometimes

known as *l'ombra*. It consists of a small glass of wine and a bite or two of *cicheti* (tapas-like salty offerings, perhaps anchovies, olives, or tiny fried fish). *Cicheti* comes from the Latin *"ciccus"* (small quantity). The term *ombra* means shade. Supposedly, long ago purveyors of wine moved their carts around the *piazza* to keep their wine cool in the shade.

The world has long wondered why the pasta-eating Italians don't get fat. The answers are portion control and no snacking in between meals. Since Italians don't eat while walking (another Food Rule) the consumption of snacks is naturally controlled to a large extent. Italian mothers do the rest.

Some will say that the snack prohibition is a thing of the past and sadly they are correct. With both mothers and fathers at work, latchkey kids are enjoying fast food lunches (a.k.a. snacks) and illicit snacks at any time in the afternoon. Although you will rarely see an Italian child walking with a can of Coke in his hand, the frequent sight of chubby children tells a story of its own.

DID YOU KNOW?

Italians denote small things by adding the singular *-ina* or *-ino* or the plural *–ine* or *–ini* on to the end of the word. A tiny snack would therefore become *merendina*. Italian expert on food and culture, Massimo Montanari, postulates that the more frequent use of the diminutive *merendina* has the effect of "de-ritualizing" the two daily breaks for "well-deserved refreshment" and creating a culture of tiny snacks or snacking that by its very nature can be done at any time, instead of the traditional times for *merenda*. So those candy bars at the cash register of every coffee bar are possibly becoming less for tourists and more for those Italians with ever-expanding waistlines.

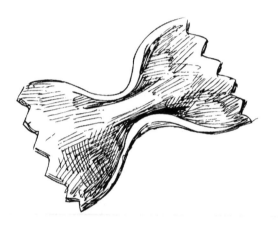

ITALIANS DON'T SNACK - THEY EAT NUTELLA

Italians stay thin (at least, in the near past), because they follow two of the Italian Food Rules: 1) No Eating While Walking; and 2) No Snacking. But then there is Nutella.

Nutella (for those who live in another universe) is a creamy chocolate-hazelnut confection that spreads like peanut butter (a food that hasn't ever gained a foothold in the Italian cupboard). The Ferrero chocolate company created Nutella as a special *merenda* (an afternoon refreshment) for children to replace the milk- or water- or wine-soaked slice of bread sprinkled with sugar that was offered up by most mothers prior to 1950. Nutella was marketed as a healthy alternative because of the protein from the hazelnuts.

Nutella only made an appearance as an after-school snack because during World War II in Italy there was an exorbitant tax on rare cocoa beans that almost destroyed the Italian chocolate industry. In

1944, Ferrero (then a bakery in the Piemonte region where hazelnuts were plentiful) created a chocolate-like mixture made of 71.5% hazelnut paste and 19.5% chocolate. At first it was marketed as *gianduia*, a tiny wrapped morsel. But children tended to throw the bread away and just eat the candy. Ferrero remade the concoction as a spread in a small jar.

After the war ended and chocolate was still expensive and in short supply, Ferrero's *Supercrema* was the most popular chocolate substitute. Children would go to the local store with a slice of bread in hand for a smear of Ferrero's spread, costing 5 lire (less than a penny). These children were hooked and Nutella (the name came in 1963, emphasizing the nut, not the chocolate) became part of the Italian food culture.

Today, the main ingredients of Nutella are sugar and palm oil, followed by hazelnut, cocoa solids and skimmed milk. Italians will still argue that eating Nutella is not "snacking" because it is only eaten on bread as a *merenda* at 4pm...or in crepes at the beach...or for a special filling for a weekend breakfast pastry...or on a spoon, whenever.

DID YOU KNOW?

In the United States, a New Jersey mother and a California mother took Ferrero USA to court in February 2011, in two separate cases, claiming that

Nutella was deceptively marketed, advertised, and sold in the United States as a "healthy" and "nutritious" food. The court documents claimed Nutella's marketing and advertising was misleading because it claimed that "Nutella is a "wholesome" food product and can be served as part of a "balanced" and "nutritious breakfast," but "omits that the nutritional value claimed, if any, is not derived from Nutella, but is instead derived from other foods or drinks (e.g., whole grain breads, fruit and milk), which are advertised to be consumed along with Nutella." They went on to say that Nutella's marketing claims were false and misleading because "they omit that Nutella contains high levels of saturated fat, the consumption of which has been shown to increase the blood cholesterol levels" and "they omit that Nutella contains over 55% processed sugar, the consumption of which has been shown to cause type 2 diabetes and other serious health problems."

In September 2012, it was announced that Ferrero USA had settled with the class action claimants for just over $3 million (estimated payout to claimants, now numbering in the thousands, is $4 to $20).

A lawsuit against Nutella would never happen in Italy.

NO ALL-YOU-CAN-EAT BUFFETS

If you come across an all-you-can-eat-buffet in Italy, you have made a rare sighting and are probably at a tourist trap (bad food) or a hotel restaurant (not necessarily bad food, but not served in an Italian manner). An all-you-can-eat-buffet breaks the following Italian Food Rules: 1) Menu Rules (separate plates for each dish, served in a specified order), 2) Pasta is Not a Side Dish, 3) No Eating Bread with Pasta, and 4) Don't Pass the Gravy (a variant in this case–don't mix the sauces).

Italians don't quite know how to act when faced with a buffet table loaded with foods that are usually regarded as appetizers, first dishes (pasta or risotto), or entrées, along with a bunch of side dishes. First, they are not sure if they should select only one food, return to their seats and eat it, thus following the rules that govern the mixing of flavors on one plate. Second, they don't know whether it is proper to eat pasta before an appetizer. Third, they don't know when bread should come into play

135

in the meal. And finally, Italians aren't sure that the platters are going to be refilled, so they tend to rush the table.

There is an "Italian" food chain in the U.S. that serves a dish called "Tour of Italy" that is a plate of "Homemade Lasagna, Lightly Breaded Chicken Parmigiana, and Creamy Fettuccine Alfredo." It adds up to 1,450 calories, 33 grams of saturated fat, and 3,830 milligrams of sodium. It is an all-you-can-eat buffet on a plate. And it breaks all of the above-mentioned Italian Food Rules and a couple more: 1) Alfredo is a name, not a pasta sauce, and 2) no Parmesan cheese on breaded chicken.

American Thanksgiving in Italy creates a similar situation to a loaded buffet table. In late November, Americans start searching for a whole turkey to roast (hard to find in any Italian market because the butcher usually cuts up the large fowl into easy to cook pieces–a stuffed, roast turkey is not an Italian dish). Whether the bird is found or not, the invitations go out. The Americans on the guest list all bring a side dish, perhaps a traditional Thanksgiving recipe or an Italian one. The Italians bring wine, chocolates or flowers. There is too much food for the normal table so another is set up nearby. Now it becomes a Thanksgiving buffet.

I remember my first Thanksgiving in Italy. The guest list contained eight Americans and two Italians. One of the Italians had experienced Thanksgiving in the U.S. and knew the drill. The other was a retired executive of a famous Italian luxury brand and though he had lived in New York for years, he had never before experienced Thanksgiving dinner. As could be expected, the Americans descended on the buffet table (in this case, the island in the open kitchen) with gusto, loading our plates with a slice of turkey, chestnut and mushroom stuffing, mashed potatoes, Parmesan creamed spinach, a couple of liver pâté *crostini*, some rare cranberry sauce, small polenta muffins, dinner rolls and turkey gravy poured over the potatoes and meat.

The Italian Thanksgiving aficionado scooped small portions of what she would consider to be appetizers from two or three platters, carefully segregating them to different areas on her plate. She sat down and finished each completely, before she went back to get small servings of turkey, mashed potatoes and stuffing. The retired Italian executive– a Thanksgiving newbie–looked in horror at the heaped plates of the Americans, took a couple of crostini and sat down. He ate them and went back to get turkey and mashed potatoes, but no gravy. He finished that, cleaned his plate with small piece of a dinner roll and went back for a taste of stuffing and some green beans. This was a man, like most Italians, who would never consider dining at an all-you-can-eat buffet.

WHAT GOES TOGETHER – TOMATO, MOZZARELLA, & BASIL

Probably the most famous food or ingredient pairing in Italy is that of fresh tomato, mozzarella cheese, and fresh basil. More than any other country, Italy prides itself in being able to pair not only wine with food, but also ingredient to ingredient– food to food.

Fresh, creamy, barely salty, mozzarella cuts the acid/sweet taste of sliced vine-ripened tomatoes. Add a sprig of fresh basil to provide an accent and you have the perfect dish, known throughout the world as *Caprese*. All that is needed is a splash of extra virgin olive oil and a bit of salt and fresh cracked black pepper.

In texture this combination is also compatible as the soft mushiness of the cheese vies with the crisp crunch of the tomato.

There can be no compromise on the pairing of ingredients in *Caprese*. Salty hard aged parmesan cannot be substituted for fresh mozzarella. Bland zucchini can't take the place of ripe tomatoes. In fact, the somewhat green, watery, traveled-a-thousand-miles tomatoes found in the U.S., or canned tomatoes, or even peeled tomatoes, cannot take the place of a mature sweet, vine-ripened, small- to medium-sized tomato. Oregano or thyme or rosemary or any other herb–even dried basil–cannot be substituted for fresh green leaves of basil, preferably growing in a pot on your windowsill.

Finally, the look of *Caprese* is quintessential Italy. *Tri-colore*–red, white and green–the colors of the Italian flag.

WHAT GOES TOGETHER –
PROSCIUTTO & MELON

The second most famous Italian food pairing is prosciutto and melon. Prosciutto, pink, salty and dry, is the perfect wrap for the orange, sweet, juicy cantaloupe.

Serve the melon peeled and sliced in long crescents with one slice of prosciutto wrapped around each piece to be eaten with a knife and fork. Or wrap a small cube or ball of melon in a tiny sack of prosciutto for perfect finger food.

The melon must be in season and as sweet as can be. Prosciutto is always available and it is a matter of taste whether the famous Prosciutto di Parma is selected or the saltier Tuscan variety from the *Cinta Sinese* pork is desired.

As with all Italian ingredient pairings, no substitutes will do. Don't wrap a slice of baked Virginia ham or of roasted *prosciutto di Praga* around a spear of watermelon or a piece of green honeydew melon. The taste will be wrong. The texture will be

141

wrong, and the color combination will not delight the Italian eye.

DID YOU KNOW?

Eating melons without the prosciutto is considered somewhat dangerous to Italians. It comes down to an issue of digestion, as many things do in regard to the Italian Food Rules. If a "cold" food, like melon, is eaten without a "hot" balancing food, like a salty meat or spicy chili peppers, the body is "chilled", which leads to the dreaded *congestione*, or at least, indigestion.

There is historical proof for this claim. In July 1471, Pope Paul II died after a dinner consisting of three cantaloupes. The melons were to blame. In 1602, Giacomo della Porta, the architect of another pope, died after reportedly eating too much cantaloupe and watermelon, causing fatal indigestion when his organs became chilled.

WHAT GOES TOGETHER – SALAME & FIGS

Salty and sweet of the highest degree meet in the pairing of figs with *salame*. This is the perfect snack or *antipasto*. It's a finger food–either roll up the juicy fig in a thin slice of *salame* and pop it in your mouth or, if the in-laws are invited, you may wish to pre-wrap the figs, skewer with a toothpick, and avoid any hand to mouth ineptness.

Don't get fancy here in your selection of *salame*. A simple cured variety large enough to wrap a fig is all you need. Avoid truffled salame or a wine infused variety. If you want to be a bit bold, try *salame di cinghiale*–wild boar *salame*.

It must be *salame*. Prosciutto is too bland. Baked ham is just wrong.

Rachael Ray promotes a recipe with cooked "salami and fig preserves". That's American, not Italian. Italians do not heat up their fabulous hand-made, long-cured, perfect-as-they-are *salami*, except if they are adding *salame piccante* to a *pizza diavola*, but only then and there isn't going to be a fig in sight.

Wait for fresh fig season. Italians don't settle for fig preserves. Many Italians will skin the fig, but it is not strictly necessary if they've been given a good wash or if you are lucky enough to have your own fig tree and a convenient *salame* and a sharp knife.

DID YOU KNOW?

The word "salami" used by English-speakers, is the plural form of the Italian word *"salame"*. In English it does not matter if there are one or two encased, cured meats or a bunch of slices ready to be wrapped around figs, it's still salami. In Italy, it matters: If you want two long uncut encased, cured meats hanging from the butcher's ceiling, you ask for *"due salami"*. If you want about ten thin slices to go around your ten small figs, ask for *"un etto di salame"* (100 grams of *salame*).

WHAT GOES TOGETHER – FRESH FAVA BEANS & PECORINO

Hannibal Lecter made fava beans famous, but his food pairing was, to say the least…wrong. Most people think of fava beans as a banal dried legume that takes hours to cook or the forgettable part of a soup or stew. The ideal pairing of fava beans (sometimes called "broad beans") is when they are fresh and eaten with pecorino cheese.

Fresh fava beans do not have the same following in the world as they do in Italy, probably because the season is so short. Tuscans call these fava beans "*baccelli*". They are at their best only in the spring, when the pods are relatively short and the beans are small and tender. Left too long on the vine the beans grow a tough skin and they must be cooked or dried to be eatable.

Italians like to eat the slightly bitter bean with small slices of a barely-aged, but flavorful, sheep's milk cheese, called *Marzolino*, the pecorino only made in the month of March when the flocks have access to the sweetest grasses and most tender herbs.

The light green *baccelli* with their slightly sharp taste and crunchy texture make a perfect match to creamy slightly salty aromatic cheese. Sometimes the beans are left in their pods and placed in the center of the Italian table on a large platter with the small wheel of pecorino *Marzolino* on a cutting board beside it. In this manner it is a finger-food appetizer where all of the diners get to hull their own beans and slice the cheese to accompany the *baccelli*.

More commonly, the shelling happens in the kitchen where the cook cubes the cheese to about the same size as the hulled beans, and then tosses them together in a bowl with a splash of olive oil, a shake of sea salt and plenty of coarsely ground fresh black pepper. The dish is then served as an antipasto.

Next time you are in Italy in the spring, go to the closest vegetable vendor and buy a kilo of *baccelli*. Then, stop by the *latteria* and pick up a half kilo of *Marzolino*. All you need after that is a knife before you will be able to taste one of the best food pairings Italy has to offer.

DID YOU KNOW?

Historically, shepherds made *Marzolino* cheese from the season's first sheep's milk obtained when the flocks were able to go back to the pasture after the winter. *Marzolino* is the youngest of the pecorino cheeses, with a soft light skin (sometimes pale orange in color), shaped in an oval form, weighing about one pound. It has a micro-season and is only supposed to be eaten in March as the name indicates. The taste of the cheese reflects the season's first grasses and herbs eaten by the ewes. The curds are wrapped in the leaves of the cardoon, further infusing it with its famous spicy grassy flavor. *Marzolino*, was perfected in Tuscany, enjoyed by the Medici Grand Dukes, taken to Rome by Michelangelo, and two centuries earlier, immortalized by Boccaccio in the *Decameron*.

WHAT GOES TOGETHER – PEAR & PECORINO

There is an ancient Italian saying from the days when the farming system was such that 50% of the farmer's crop went to the landowner and 10% went to the church–*al contadino non far sapere quant'è buono il cacio con le pere*–don't tell the farmer how good cheese tastes with pears. Since the farmer milked the ewes, made the cheese and picked the pears, the landowners and priests had a right to fear their portions would be shorted.

One of the world's leading experts on food and culture, Massimo Montanari, wrote a 128-page book, entitled *Il Formaggio con le Pere: La Storia in un Proverbio* (Cheese with Pears: The History in a Proverb), which unravels the origin and use throughout history of the saying.

The right cheese with the right fruit is the key to Italian food pairing. The proper cheese is an aged *pecorino*, made from sheep's milk, salty with a stronger flavor than cow's milk cheese. (There are some Italians who argue for a younger creamier cheese, but they still agree that it must be *pecorino*.)

The pears must be mature, but crisp–sweet, but not mushy. Some claim Bartlett pears are best, but no one puts up much of an argument, unless you try to substitute another fruit.

This is a white on white dish because Italians *always* peel their fruit before eating it. The dish can be presented as pear crescents alternated with thin slices of *pecorino* or the pears can be halved and the *pecorino* shaved (not grated) in curls on top of the fruit or finally the pear and cheese can be cut in equal sized cubes and tossed together. One daring chef tried to solve the problem of over-ripe pears by creating a fruit sauce to spread on cheese. Try this for your Italian friends at your peril.

DON'T TOUCH THE FRUITS AND VEGETABLES

Food shoppers in the U.S. feel free to poke, prod, squeeze, thump and sniff the fruits and vegetables whether they plan to buy the produce or not. At a *fruttivendolo* stand in Italy that habit will garner you a withering look and a command to unhand the eggplant: "*Non tocchi le melanzane, per favore!*"

One of the pleasures of life in Italy is the taste of vine-ripened (or tree-ripened) fruits and vegetables. This is a major reason Italian food is so good—there are fresh local ingredients at the perfect level of ripeness. They are a feast for eye as well as the stomach. This also makes the produce delicate to the touch, even if you don't have the outsized fear of germs that most Italians have.

The Italian Food Rule: Don't Touch the Fruits and Vegetables, has its basis in both the protection of the produce and the desire to reduce the spread of disease.

The proper procedure is to approach a shopkeeper and say "*buongiorno*" followed by saying exactly what you'd like to buy. You'll have to deal with weights and/or numbers. "*Un chilo di fagiolini, per favore*"–a kilo (2.2 pounds) of green beans, please; "*Tre cipolle, per favore*"–three onions, please; or harder still for the metrically-challenged: "*Quattro etti di zucchine, per favore*"–four hectograms (400 grams) of zucchini.

It's considered rude to tell the *fruttivendola* exactly which fruit she should put in your bag. She's the expert. Locals will tell a vendor when they plan to eat their fruit and she'll use her expertise to pick those at the appropriate stage of ripeness, especially for the repeat customers she wants to keep happy. If you want ripe fruit to eat today, add clarification, "*da mangiare oggi, per favore*"–to eat today, please.

Sometimes a vendor will tell you to just go ahead and pick out your own fruit, or you can request permission by asking, "*Posso?*" (May I?). Then wait for a nod or the passing of a plastic or paper sack for your use. But just because you have permission to select your own potatoes, doesn't mean they want to see you rooting through the bin tossing your rejects hither and yon. You're expected to carefully select and touch only those items you wish to buy, unless there's obviously something wrong with them. It's all about hygiene.

You may have the luck to find the one or two produce vendors in Italy who love foreigners and take pride in providing all of their customers, new and old, with the very best fruit and vegetables they have to offer. Do not feel bad if this is not the case on the day you are shopping for figs and plums. The *ortolano* may not have your best interests at heart. It most likely has less to do with the fact that you don't speak Italian with the local accent as it has to do with the fact that you are not a regular customer and he has produce he needs to offload.

One of my most memorable experiences when I followed this Italian Food Rule to my regret came on the day I wanted to buy three large fresh porcini mushrooms. I went to a stand in Florence's *Mercato Centrale* where the vendor only sold mushrooms— the expert. There was even an example of his high quality porcini split in half exposing its firm white worm-free center.

I followed the Italian Food Rule: Don't Touch the Produce. I asked for three large porcini with stems and caps. He selected three fine looking specimens and placed them carefully in a paper bag. I trudged home with my sacks of shopping, unloaded them on the table and discovered that one of my fine mushrooms had a toothpick holding the cap to the stem and was turning slightly brown at the center. But there were no worms.

Buying groceries at an Italian supermarket is easier. You get to touch the produce, but not with your bare hands. At Coop or Esselunga or Conad, it won't be the vendor upholding the Italian Food Rule: Don't Touch the Fruits and Vegetables. It will be Italian housewives, young to very old, enforcing a subset of the Rule: Don't touch the produce without a plastic glove. A withering look from an Italian grandmother is just scary. A sarcastic comment is even more frightening.

One of the pleasures of living in Italy is shopping at the food markets. The produce is fresher and more flavorful than at the supermarket. Find an *ortolana* who treats you right and then get to know her, asking her advice about what to buy and how to cook it, greeting her even when not shopping for produce. It is a relationship that can last, seemingly, a lifetime and can save you from finding a toothpick in your porcini.

DID YOU KNOW?

You'll find plastic gloves near the plastic bags in the section with the fruits and vegetables, and you're expected to use them. This is the procedure for buying loose vegetables and fruits in a supermarket:

1) Find a plastic glove; 2) Put it on; 3) Get a plastic bag for each of your desired fruits or vegetables; 4) Select your produce from the bins; 5) Look for and remember the code on the bin's label; 6) Place your bag on the nearby scale and push the button that corresponds to the code; and 7) Wait for a printed sticker to exit the scale and paste it on outside of the bag.

If you don't follow this procedure, the checker will have to do it for you when you check out (or worse, will send you back to do it), much to the displeasure of the people in the line behind you.

Italians Eat Local and in Season

Italians eat food made from ingredients that are seasonal and produced locally. This is the basis for the quality of Italian food in Italy.

That is not to say the food is the same throughout the peninsula. The reason that there are so many discussions taking place in Italy among Italians about which region has the best bread or wine or fish or pasta sauce or *ravioli* or cheese or *bistecca* or extra virgin olive oil, is that each region produces its own ingredients locally and the recipes have been passed down for centuries. But the quality of the ingredients is uniformly superior throughout the country because Italians eat in season and use local ingredients.

Yes, fruit from South America arrives during the winter in Italy, but, by and large, the Italians don't buy the imports because their mothers have told them that you only eat citrus in the winter, apples in the fall, and strawberries in the summer.

Tomatoes do not travel thousands of miles to

Italian markets, arriving partially green and tasteless. Each type of tomato, the one selected as perfect for the recipe, arrives in season, vine-ripened and sweet (except for those specifically left slightly green for salads and those picked very early for a Tuscan fried green tomato *frittata*).

As you travel throughout Italy, do not try to order a dish that is the specialty of Venice in Rome or a recipe from Rome in a Florentine trattoria. Ask a local where to eat and what to eat. Drink the local wine–it will complement the local food. While in Italy, join the Italians in eating food made of ingredients that are in season and produced locally.

ACKNOWLEDGEMENTS

I send *mille grazie* to Wilma, who first taught Francesca, who then taught me, each and every one of these Italian Food Rules.

To Barbara and Lynette, who both love Italy, but value proper English grammar and spelling. To my dad, who argued that not everyone knows what the Italian words mean. To Francesca, again, for finding my many errors in Italian spelling and usage. Any remaining errors are mine, alone.

My heartfelt thanks to the Matera Women's Fiction Festival and Elizabeth and the Brainstormers who have encouraged me to get the Italian Food Rules down on paper.

To Anselm Aston and Kelly Crimi for their talents, which took the manuscript from scattered pages and transformed it into a "real" book beyond my imagining.

Last but not least, to Christine Witthohn and the Book Cents Literary Agency, without whom this book would have remained floating random thoughts.

159

About the Author

Photo Credit: Ann Reavis

Five years used to be Ann Reavis' attention span for any career. She's been a lawyer, a nurse, a presidential appointee in a federal agency, a tour guide and a freelance writer. She's lived in New Mexico, Texas, California (San Francisco Bay Area), Michigan and Washington, DC.

But fifteen years ago Ann fell in love with Italy and has been traveling to and from Florence ever since. She shares her thoughts on Florence, Tuscany, and all things Italian in a travel and food blog–TuscanTraveler.com.

Made in the USA
Middletown, DE
16 August 2018